Love and Forgiveness

A Workbook for Self Healing
and Healing Relationships

Leonard M. Shaw, M.S.W., A.C.S.W.

♥ *Love and Forgiveness*

Price: $10.00
*Audio and video tapes also
available, see p. 109*

Cover design by Richard Hess
Book design by Linda Sawaya

Dedicated to my wife, Dana
My willing companion in the Universe of Love

❤ ACKNOWLEDGMENTS

There are so many people to thank and appreciate for their love and support that I will list most of them alphabetically.

First of all, my parents, who gave me and taught me so much: Leonard and Velma Shaw, Fay and Howard Sweeney.

My Family:
Dana Shaw
Virginia Bakken
Marlene Hilsenberg
Kathleen and Peggy Howard
Ed and Sylvia Odion
Anne Shaw
Cynthia Shaw
Mathew and Juleen Shaw
Eric Zinda

My Teachers and Friends:
Ian Alger
Ed Askren III
Syd Banks
David Berg
Steve Bogen
Thomas and Doris Bungardt
Carol Byron
Cal Capener
Ram Dass
Alex Edelstein
John Enright
Joe and Mardi Goodman
Dave Gronewold
Frank Hammer
Ron Hanna
Bill Hanna
Neils Hoffmeyer
Ben Joshua Jaffe
Birthe Jakobsen
Jerry Jampolsky
Otto Larsen
Bob Macdonald
Roger Mills
Arnold Patent
Fritz Perls
George Pransky
Ric Sanchez
Jerry Stoltenberg
Art Stolz
Ted Teather

And my clients, with whom I have shared my love, my learning and my mistakes. Please forgive me for my mistakes and take my best offerings with you.

❤ FORWARD

In seminars, I have an informal and personal way of present-
ing this wisdom and that seems to make it quite useful and
practical for people. When I transcribe that part of the seminar
into writing (which is what we have attempted with much of this
workbook) it sometimes comes out wordy and/or hard to
follow. In editing I have tried to keep the informal and personal
flavor that people seem to find so useful. Some of you may find
it too informal and some of you may find it too stiff. And, of
course, what would I say but, "please forgive me, and focus on
my love for you that is expressed through this book."

The length of this book is a little humbling to me. I have held
a prejudice since graduate school, that most non-fiction books
could be reduced to 40 pages of nitty-gritty. Perhaps we can
look at this as three short books combined into one.

*Available on tape See p. 109

3. Appendix (Compilation of Themes Written in Past Eight Years)

For the impatient and/or action oriented, you may wish to turn to section two, Exercises for Self-Healing.

❤ THE FRIDAY NIGHT INTRODUCTION

Some of you have heard me talk before and are hearing this for the second or third time or more. Others are here for the first time. I just want you to know that even if you have heard this before, you should be open to the possibility that with my saying exactly the same thing I have said before, something will shift in you that has not shifted before. It is the sort of wisdom we need to be reminded of all our lives.

And, when I talk to you about this, I see things about my own life even as I talk to you, things I had not quite seen before...or I have a break-through in letting go or forgiving myself. This wisdom is like a Sufi–tale you get what you are ready to get when you read it. You might read it six days or six months later and get something else from it.

Now, I will tell you just a little bit about how I got here because, though I have been doing therapy for twenty-five years, I have only been doing this therapy and teaching for eight years. I have always been a searching, pioneering sort of therapist or teacher. I am always looking for the most impactful, efficient, intense short-term therapy or teaching tools. I started out as a nondirective Freudian–which lasted about three years–and then became existential and then practiced and taught Gestalt for about twelve years.

Then around eight years ago, I saw two friends start to change in ways that I never thought I would see. Each one of them had character armor that was so tough that I never thought they would soften up. But I saw them softening up. Every few months, on their way to Canada, they would stay all night at my house and I would think, "What is going on with these guys? Anything that affects them this way I want to look into."

That was about eight years ago—I started looking into it, listening to tapes and studying it. The source of it was a man named Sidney Banks. He had never studied psychology, religion or philosophy or anything like that. Sid had had a kind of spontaneous enlightenment... and he was affecting my friends in a very profound way. So I studied this wisdom for about a year and thought I was practicing it.

There are some pitfalls to this—one part of you wants to learn how to let go, surrender, forgive and evolve and be this effortlessly happy, love-filled person, while the other part of you wants to learn how to be a slicker version of you with your games and your rackets. There is no need to beat yourself up about it. You would just get stuck. You just need to notice that one part of you wants to polish your rackets while this other part of you wants to surrender. The ego hates the word surrender.

Well, I studied this wisdom for about a year. I thought I was practicing it, teaching it...and I really was not. I had not surrendered to it. One day I said, "Leonard, you are just afraid— you're afraid that if you really practice and teach this, if you really surrender to this, that, number one, your clients will get so much so fast they won't need you anymore, and you'll go out of business—or, number two, they'll think you're so airy fairy and far out, that you don't know what you're talking about, and they will not want to come back and work with you."

Well, I discovered that my clients were always much more ready to hear this wisdom than I was to share it. I would share it and all the time my ego would be whispering to me, "Don't say that! Don't say that! They'll think you're stupid or foolish or naive..."

8

But I would just force myself to say it anyway. And my clients would have these wonderful breakthrough experiences. After awhile—(it took two or three years)—I knew I would always go through that process, so I just relaxed about it.

The same thing happened the other day when Andy Barry interviewed me on the radio. There were points where my ego would shout inside my head, "Don't say that, Leonard. People will think it's too sweet, innocent, naive, airy fairy, too outlandish." So, even tonight, as I tell you some of these things, once in awhile my ego will say, "Don't say that!" But I feel I must say these things in order to give you my best. To give you the best I have to offer, I have to say some things that make my ego nervous.

And I *am* going to say them and you—you are going to have a little debate in the back of your head: "Nyah, nyah, nyah, nyah, what's this, what's that? What does he mean by that? And how can I turn this into a technique or some thing?" You see, that is the other thing. You want to turn this wisdom into a technique in order to manipulate more goodies out of the universe—and I would go through that as a therapist. In a therapy session, I could tell when I was getting scared because I would try to do what I did in the last interview—that had worked so well. I would try to do exactly the same thing in the next interview.

Well, that is using it as a technique. It gets limited results that way. So just notice when your ego wants to use it that way, and then reach for your higher self, your loving, forgiving, surrendering self. When I was the Gestalt expert, I felt very safe. I had introduced Gestalt to the Puget Sound area when people still thought it dangerous and irresponsible. After teaching it for twelve years, and guest lecturing in ten or fifteen departments at the University of Washington and the medical school, I felt safe in my expertise. Well, when you practice the wisdom I am sharing with you tonight, you are constantly a beginner and it drives the ego nuts. I went from being the Gestalt expert to being a spiritual toddler.

But if you keep practicing it, you realize there is a freshness that goes with it. The simplest things in life are so fantastic and nourishing. It is like "Zen mind, beginners mind." Every experience has the potential for being a virginal experience for you. You walk out your door and see the geraniums there like you are looking at them for the first time. And they seem like a miracle to you. The red of their blossoms have such depth!

And your life *is* full of miracles. You are surrounded by miracles that you take for granted every day. These miracles could be nourishing you tremendously. In fact, there is so much love and abundance and nourishment surrounding you that you actually have to work at shutting it out. It takes a lot of extra energy to focus on lack–looking at the glass as half empty rather than half full.

And it is just a function of your little mind. It is just the way your ego works. We all have a little mind and a big mind. In your little mind you ruminate and stew, you manipulate, you dwell on the past and try to predict the future. The little mind runs on fear, insecurity and scarcity consciousness. Yet we all have a big mind and in your big mind you know everything I am telling you is true, that we are all brothers and sisters, that we are all in this together and that the main reason you are here on the planet is to give and receive love and to expand.

All this other stuff, like whether you wear a black shirt or a purple shirt or drive a bus or do brain surgery, is not nearly as big a deal as you think. In your big mind you know you are not your body, are not your emotions, are not your ego...that you are something grand and mysterious beyond all that, something more than we can understand. You know all this in your big mind, but you are still addicted to figuring things out, to analyzing and predicting the future. Your ego is going to try to figure things out while you sit here tonight. And that is all right, that is just how the ego works. What I am talking about is beyond words, actually, and beyond understanding. I use these words to point you in the direction of this wisdom, to say "it feels like this," or "here are some of the ways to shift from your little mind to your big mind."

So, anyway, after studying and thinking about this wisdom for about a year, I just surrendered to it and it was very scary. I guess I will tell this story because...it is important to know what it feels like to go through a significant death and rebirth.

I had postponed one of my weekend seminars and went to San Francisco to do the seminar my two friends were leading. By now they had studied this wisdom a great deal and practiced with Sid. Now they were doing their own seminars. It was the kind of seminar where they would talk a little bit and we would share a little bit. A lot of us in the seminar would just share little examples of how this wisdom had affected our lives.

At the end of the weekend, they took me and another close mutual friend aside and said, "We just want you to know that everything you two were sharing this weekend was ego." And I just thought, "Oh, God, why is it whenever I get close to somebody, they need to find things wrong with me?" (which is one of my old tapes.) Then I looked at George sitting on this log and he...he just looked so innocent. And I took a deep breath and said, "You're absolutely right." When I said that, it was like all this character armor I had, just went ***splxxcb***—just gently crumbled and sank to the ground. Like when a building is demolished and they put barely enough dynamite in it to blow it up and it just crumbles to the ground. That is what I felt was going on inside me.

Because, when you let go of the past, when you let go of these old tapes, you just do not know who you are going to be. You have been "doing this" and "being that" most of your life. It is scary to let go of your old tapes and reactions, even though you know they cripple and limit you.

When you were two days, two weeks, two years old, you made conclusions about life and intimacy and feelings and vulnerability, these limiting, negative conclusions about how life works...and you know what?—Once you made those conclusions, you spent the rest of your life proving they were correct. Your ego would rather be right about those conclusions than let you have an effortless, love-filled existence.

And that is one of the most powerful statements I will tell you all night. If you really see that, get a glimpse of it, how you made these limiting conclusions when you were very young and then spent the rest of your life proving them correct...then it will have been well worth your coming to this seminar.

Like "God, why is it when I let anyone else get close to me, they need to find things wrong with me?"—That was a hard one for me to let go of. It is like we all have these tapes that follow us around, playing with the help of our ego, whispering into our ear, "Fall back into me...good old familiar me...you know this is true." Be it ever so shitty, there is no place like home. Two hundred times a day you have a chance to take a stand for fear or love. Two hundred times a day, while these old tapes whisper "come with me...come with me..." and you just fall back into your ego.

So, anyway, I went back to Seattle and ran my seminar the

following weekend and I had one of my toughest clients in the seminar—a guy who had this grim approach to life. He was a guy who would go home every Friday night and pull the shades and spend the weekend feeling miserable and shut out the world. His girlfriend had abandoned him and so on. Well, the guy just laughed the whole weekend. I would talk about this wisdom and he would just start laughing. And he was never able to take himself so seriously again. Once in awhile he would still go home and pull the shades, but he had to laugh at himself while he was doing it. He knew what he was doing and he would still do it. But he would not take himself so seriously. That is the thing—once you really see what I am talking about, you can never take your problems as seriously again. You know on some level you are making them all up.

You see, life is just an interpretation—a movie you are making up. You think it is happening to you, but actually you cast the characters, you control the lighting, the volume, you pick the background—I am not saying you can choose whether it rains or shines tomorrow, although I am open to the possibility—but when you get up tomorrow, whether it is raining or sunny, you give it an interpretation. You could be grateful or you could be complaining. There are some real powerful ramifications to what I am saying.

One of the most powerful is that your parents made some mistakes with you, and you gave those mistakes interpretations. Usually it is something like they do not love me as much as my little brother, or they have it in for me, they did not really want me, or I was probably adopted. You just gave it a negative interpretation and made it significant to you. But underneath all that, in fact, the only reason they behaved the way they did was because they were afraid. The more destructive they were, the more frightened they were and...underneath all that fear, underneath all that fearful behavior, they loved you and wanted the best for you. Even if they did not know it themselves, even if they thought you were a complete pain in the ass, waste of time and they were sorry they ever had you. Honestly, underneath all that fearful behavior on their part is a deeper part of them that they were out of touch with that **loves you** and **wants the best for you**. And that love has surrounded you your whole life. It surrounds you right now and you can tune in to it just like switching a channel on your television.

And if you do tune into it, it will change you forever.

Now this does not mean that you will want to go hang around your parents if they are abusive or alcoholics or something like that...if they are into some negative, addictive behavior like constantly criticizing you. I would not recommend you hang around them for very long periods of time at all. You may not even want to see them. The point is, you can tune into this love I am talking about and let go of that interpretation where you took their behavior personally. You can forgive them for their ignorant behavior, let go of them and you will never be the same. You can tell yourself, "My father loves me very much, my mother loves me very much." And in some way that I do not understand, and I doubt anyone else does either, there is some deep empowering healing that takes place when you focus on this love and give up this old interpretation that you have had since childhood. It really transforms the quality of your existence.

Any questions about anything so far?

   Q. Yes...The question is, "What if this old tape is deeply rooted within you, just embedded—as if when you came out of your mother's womb and they rested you on her belly and she took one look at you and went 'eeyuck' and

has been doing that ever since?" That would be a deeply embedded tape.

A. What I am saying still applies. It may mean you have a bigger job of surrendering to do—and there is one thing you can do. I will be sharing a powerful healing process with people this weekend. I do not have time to go into it now, but it involves your making a list. You make a list of things that your mother— just using your mom as an example—you make a whole list of all the negative tapes, all the terrible, painful experiences, all the garbage she ever dumped on you, all the painful things she ever inflicted on you, or the terrible attitudes she demonstrated in her relationship with your father. You make a list of all this garbage and you take this list and then you ask this question: "Am I willing for everything on this list to become a source of expansion, power, peace, healing, and affirmation in my life? If you can say yes, you are willing, even though you do not have the faintest idea of what I am talking about, even though it seems improbable, impossible, and implausible, if you are willing to let it happen, then we can do some fantastic things with that list that are very healing and empowering. (This exercise follows later in the book.)

But, if you cannot say yes, then you need to say, "I refuse to forgive my mother for her ignorant behavior towards me no matter what it costs me—and that just happens to be who I am tonight here and now. I do not know how long I will be this way, but that is who I am right now..." The truth sets you free, you see, (even when you are stuck). If you can tell the truth without beating yourself up, you can open the door for a little movement. So, no matter how deeply embedded the pain, or the old tapes are, the wisdom I am sharing with you tonight is embedded even deeper. So, for some of you, even while your ego is analyzing and debating what I am saying, do not be surprised if there is this other part of you that just has this peaceful feeling about what I am saying. Sometimes people just sit there and cry, tears come down their cheeks, because they feel like they are coming home, as if they have been waiting all their lives to be reminded of this. It is *that* deep within you, even deeper than any tapes you got from your parents. I tell people, "Look, even if your mom just got off the bus, gave birth to you, dropped you in a garbage can and got back on the bus, this wisdom still applies." Because there are no exceptions to the wisdom even though everyone's ego is thinking of exceptions all the time.. That is the way the ego operates. It is okay if you do not transform your life, but I really encourage all of you tonight, to be open to the possibility you could get it just from this discussion. You may not even need to go through the whole seminar. You could get it tonight and change forever.

And you will still make mistakes, slip back and get into righteous indignation. But then you can say, "Oh, I slipped— I am back to my old indignation.—Well, then, this mistake is going to give me an even stronger connection to love and forgiveness. I am going to take a stronger stand." So, even your mistakes can contribute to your peace and power. Your mistakes always contribute if you allow them.

I will tell you something else the ego does not understand and hates to hear: *every negative experience is as positive as it is negative*, and usually more so, if your ego will just let go of its conclusion about it. (I guarantee you that every mistake, every disaster has the potential to contribute to your life at least as much as, or even more than, the *negative* experience of it would.) But remember, our ego would rather be right about what a disaster it is than be open to the benefits of the disaster.

Q. I was wondering where this teaching comes from, if it has a name—you haven't put a name on it?

A. Well, I do not know what to call it either—love and forgiveness, ego-death and surrender—it is everything that Jesus and Buddha tried to teach people, everything Mohammed tried to teach. It has been around a long time. Unfortunately, people get a hold of it, run it through their ego and then beat other people up with it.

When I was a kid, one of my best friend's parents were strict, religious people. They would say these stern things to me and sometimes take me to their church. I would hear these stern things and it would be a really schizophrenic experience for me. I felt there was something important to what they were saying, but I felt strange about it. In the last eight years, it has become very clear to me that they were talking the talk, but not walking the walk. They were speaking words of wisdom, but they were not practicing Christ consciousness in the way they spoke to me. That is where the confusion came in. A lot of so-called religious people use this wisdom to manipulate people and make them feel bad. And you will find yourself doing the same thing at times. When you do, the sooner you tell the truth about it, the better you will feel.

It does not matter to me if you talk about God or not—for some people it fits, for others it does not. What really matters is if you practice this love and forgiveness wisdom. If you practice recognizing that everyone is your brother and sister and that underneath their fearful behavior ***they love you and want the best for you***—(even if they do not know it) a peace, abundance and personal power will come into your life.

If you practice living in that state, taking a stand for love, for forgiveness, and for commitment, you will never regret it. You practice it and your life becomes fantastic! It becomes so beautiful, abundant, flowing and effortless compared to the struggle we usually make of it. So, it is walking the walk that matters, not talking the talk, and, since it is beyond words anyway, you can give it any name you want...but the name is not as important as surrendering to it and living it on a day-to-day basis.

Q. But are you not setting yourself up to expect some things from other people when you say to yourself that other people love and care for you, want the best for you, even though they are behaving in ways that are quite negative or addictive?

A. Real good point. If you are expecting change, you are in trouble. If you are using this wisdom to try and change them, bring out the best in them, you are in trouble. The key is to practice this without any expectation. It does bring out the best in people, but not as a technique or manipulation. The word 'expect' is tricky and paradoxical. I really expect the best from people, but I am not holding my breath waiting for it to happen. I look for the best, but if something else shows up, I try to let it be okay. There is a powerful line in the Course of Miracles that says, "when a brother acts insanely, we can only heal him by seeing the sanity in him."

Now, it does not mean you deny the insanity or try to avoid it—you just focus on the sanity and love in people. What happens is that you walk around with your heart on your sleeve. You walk around in this open vulnerable state that makes the ego nervous. Here is another statement the ego hates to hear: Your vulnerability is your source of invulnerability. Now the way most people live is that they guard their heart carefully and about once every eighteen months, someone breaks it and it is a big disaster.

If you go around in this state of love and forgiveness, your heart gets broken twenty, thirty times a day. And it is no big deal.

Now, it sounds a little scary, but the more you practice it, the easier life gets. So you do expect the best in people, but not in a negative way. It is not like you hold back until they show their best. You just expect the best from people, and practice loving them no matter how they happen to behave.

You see this sometimes in mental health hearings when someone has been institutionalized. The patient is treated like a human being, treated with respect, and he or she often drops the psychotic behavior they had on the ward. They come in and sit down with the judge and therapists and they are treated with respect and they behave very normally. You do not even know how disturbed the person is until he glances around the room and states, "I built this place."

Now my two friends, George and Roger, have taught this wisdom in psychiatric hospitals or locked wards with so-called crazy people and some of those people showed such strength and maturity and love, that it amazed everybody. I do not know if anyone here has worked in a mental hospital, but sometimes you feel the patients are more sane than the staff. The hospitals tend to identify the patients as sick and when patients start behaving in a loving, mature, open fashion, it sometimes makes the staff quite nervous. Because, in a lot of ways, the patients are already more open, honest, and vulnerable, whereas the staff are contained, manipulative, guarding their images, and cautious. So, in some ways, crazy people are already closer to this wisdom than the staff of their hospital.

Also, kids catch on faster because they have not lived in the universe of fear as long as adults have. Kids catch on quickest, adults have a harder time, and mental health professionals often have the hardest time of all.

Q. My parents seem loving, but I really have trouble trusting it or letting it in.

A. Most people avoid their feelings—some by understating or hiding them, some by overstating them. Possibly people in your family overstate, are a little gushy or mushy. So that is one possible source of the difficulty you describe. It is not the most common, but if true, then you need to practice forgiving them for overstating their feelings, because they are afraid to sit still for the exact vulnerability of who they are, how they feel and how much they love you.

Another possibility is that your family dynamics are like a family who have a member with some kind of traumatic illness or difficulty or limitation. Sometimes people feel this way when they are a twin and their twin died at birth or they had a sibling that died. There are a lot of possibilities to why you are not surrendering to your parents' love.

Maybe they had expectations to go with it. Maybe they love you a lot, but you are never quite good enough. They are often suggesting something slightly more, slightly different than who you are. "Why aren't you going to graduate school?" Sometimes they are more subtle: "Have you ever thought of going to graduate school?"

In some ways, you might be better off if you had slightly crazy parents, because then, when you were around seven or eight or twelve, you could have realized that "Yeah, my mom's kinda crazy, isn't she?" You get help with your reality testing that way.

Other times you have parents who seem like the nicest parents in the world. Everybody loves them and tells you what great parents you have, but you always have this slightly grungy feeling. You do not know why, because it is a very, very subtle "not quite good enough" feeling. So we need to know a little more about the family dynamics to know exactly why you have difficulty surrendering to their love.

But no matter what is going on, you deserve their love and if they are not giving it to you in a way that is totally believable, all you need to do is forgive them for that and realize they are that way because they are afraid and you can still love them. You can still surrender to this love underneath their fearful behavior. And, if they have great expectations, slight or subtle expectations, forgive them for that.

Q. You use the word 'fear' and I do not understand how you are using it.

A. Well, for about seventeen years, as a therapist, I thought that basically there were all these different kinds of negative states or feelings. For example, ***anger, jealousy, manipulation, intimidation, seductiveness***, and more. What I have realized in the last eight years is that there are really only two emotions— love and fear. That is all there is. Love and Fear.

So if someone is sending you anything other than love, you can know the bottom line is fear. Underneath all the B.S., all the dances, all the manipulations, is nothing but fear.

And, if you start practicing this wisdom, you find life becomes much easier. There will be a lot of situations where you would have reacted negatively or judgmentally toward people, where now you find yourself saying something really compassionate. Instead of "Who's your supervisor? I want to complain about the way you are treating me", you now say something loving like, "Sometimes dealing with the public gets really difficult, doesn't it?"

When people are in the universe of fear, one part of them—their deeper, more loving self—is hoping you will not get sucked in, while their ego is doing all it can to suck you in.

As you practice this wisdom, you tend to bring out the best in people. Agitated clerks often mellow out and become quite pleasant and useful. However, it is best if you use this wisdom for your own peace of mind, personal power, and healing. If you use it to "fix," change, or manipulate others, it will often backfire or turn your life a bit gray or shallow.

In my private practice I work with some very psychiatrically sophisticated people—people who have had a lot of psycho-therapy or have taken powerful seminars—and yet they have this conflict in their lives and they do not understand why. They are practicing all of this wonderful wisdom, but they have this unhappiness with their mate. What it invariably boils down to is that they are using this wisdom to subtly make their mate wrong, to try to change or manipulate their mate. It turns to pain and hurt every time.

To fully use this wisdom, you need to surrender to it. It is a surrender of the heart. You can tell when you have forgiven someone, really forgiven someone, because you feel this peaceful connection with them and an appreciation for what they gave you and who they are. It does not matter what or how terrible a disaster they helped you create in your life, there is always some benefit to it and when you have forgiven them, you will start getting the benefits of the disaster.

So all negative emotion and behaviors come from fear. When you can:

1. See this fear, under the surface-behavior;
2. Remind yourself that deep down we are all brothers and

sisters and love each other (even if we do not consciously know it); and

3. Forgive people for their ignorant behavior towards you, then a peace and power will come over your life that will amaze you.

Q. About having a peaceful connection—and practicing forgiveness—I have reached a point where I have stopped and I do not know how to get back on...I do not feel I have had a peaceful connection with anyone for months. Do you have a suggestion? Can I get it back?

A. Well, there are a lot of different tools I use. I do not know which one would touch you. One statement I use that is really powerful is, "There is a solution to this that will delight everybody." The ego cannot stand it, but it is a very powerful statement. Another thing is to ask yourself, "What am I afraid of?" or "Who have I not forgiven?" Does anything come to mind? You don't have to say it out loud, but when I ask that, does anything come to mind? (The person asking the original question was blushing and smiling at this point.)

Well, there is where your work is to be done.

Q. Well, I know where it is to be done and I know I am unforgiving and I know I am stuck there...and to admit it right now made me feel better.

A. If it makes you feel better, that is a good sign. You probably need to say, "I refuse to forgive Dad (or mate or somebody) for their ignorant behavior towards me no matter what it costs me." Just breathe... It is okay. If anybody wants to help her, just take a deep breath. That is all you have to do. And do not beat yourself up for being unforgiving or you could be stuck there for a long time.

Q. What happens if you forgive people who do not

forgive—people who hold grudges, who like to hold grudges?

A. What happens depends on what you want. If you forgive and the other person is holding a grudge, I would not recommend you hang around the person holding a grudge. But I would recommend you keep on forgiving that person. What the ego wants to do is notice they have not forgiven you and in a subtle, or not so subtle way, judge them for not forgiving you. Your voice sounded as if you have some judgmental energy towards this person for not forgiving you. It just means this person is a special teacher for you and there is an extra lesson in life you can learn from this unforgiving person. When you forgive this unforgiving person, ***what happens is that you will be loving a part of yourself that you have been refusing to love your whole life!*** This is something that is very powerful and beyond understanding.

I repeat. When you forgive somebody that you have refused to forgive, you are actually loving a part of yourself that you have been withholding love from. We all have these experiences where we are not forgiving. All the people we ***have*** forgiven are not a problem. But often we do have a special area of un-forgiveness for certain people and it means that they are special teachers for us with a little extra something to give us.

Q. Some of these people write you off for the rest of your life...

A. Yes, and do you know what happens? They poison themselves. They are not doing anything to you. If you want to be free of it, all you have to do is forgive them. If you are still waiting for them to change, you are poisoning yourself. What is transformational is loving people exactly the way they are. This is frightening for the ego, because if you love them the way they are, the ego thinks they will burn you again. The truth is that if you love them exactly the way they are, the chances they will burn you again are actually decreased. Hanging onto your judgments increases the likelihood they will burn you again. It makes no sense to the ego which has it wired up exactly the opposite...but when you walk around in a state of judgment and unforgiveness you attract more toxic behavior into your life. You are apt to repeat the same mistakes with somebody else or that same person you feel unforgiving toward.

Q. I have a difficult time seeing that there are only two emotions, love and fear. I can see love on the positive side, but it is difficult for me to reduce anger and other negative emotions down to fear....

A. What is your objection to saying that fear is behind the other emotions? Does it not make sense or is it that it just does not fit?

Q. Well, when I get angry, I have this thought, "Underneath this is fear," but I have not been able to get in touch with what I have been afraid of, so it just does not fit.

A. Well, would you like to explore that right now?

A. Okay.

A. Tell me something that really upsets you, really makes you angry... Think of anything?

Q. Yeah— something my boyfriend does all the time...or a lot.

A. Are you willing to tell us what it is?

Q. No...

A. Well, we can work with it anyway... Your boyfriend does this chronic thing that upsets you? Do you see it yet? Sometimes people see it right away.

Q. No, I do not see what I am afraid of...

A. Whatever it is that he does, I suggest that you are ***interpreting*** it like he does not really love you, he is not really there for you, he does not prioritize your relationship. And when it is a chronic situation, what may be going on is that one of your parents was not there for you or did not prioritize your relationship and you are afraid that he is just like them. He is going to hurt you or abuse you, not be there for you—just like they were.

Q. I am not making that connection. Right now, I am in touch with some fear, I have connected with it...

A. Good...

Q. But I do not have a connection with my parents or where in my relationship with my parents that the fear is coming from—what it is that I am afraid of.... What I do not like is...my judgment about him is...that he always wants to have sex...

A. Ah...

Q. And right now I am experiencing a physical problem that seems to be related to this and I want to let go of the physical problem and I know where the work needs to take place, within me. Right now, as we are talking, I am experiencing that fear I have associated with it. I have had that fear for a long time—which is that I am afraid men always want to have sex with me, I am afraid I am going to be raped or something...but I do not have any connection to where that comes from....

A. That is okay. I am open to the possibility it does not matter.

The thing is that there are numerous things it could be from.... Now, I do not even know what you mean by "all the time," but that does not matter. If he wants to have sex all the time, one thing that would help you would be to recognize his compulsion to have sex is a manifestation of fear in him. Underneath it is some kind of fear. Your fear of having sex all the time is who knows what??? You might be afraid of being consumed in the relationship, devoured psychologically. There are some simple exercises you can do around that fear of being consumed or devoured psychologically. But the point is, whenever I have talked to anyone in a little bit of depth as you and I are doing right now, what we get to is some kind of fear—fear of being consumed, fear of being taken over, fear of loss of control, fear of being hurt, abandoned or something else.

Now, the kind of breakthrough homework that comes to mind for people like you and your boyfriend,—now this is just an example, I am not necessarily recommending this—but these transformational examples just come out of the discussions automatically—is for you to take two weeks where you have sex all the time and just surrender to it and take another two weeks where you have no sex and he surrenders to it.

Obviously, you are both attracted to each other because you fit each other's fears perfectly. This sort of thing happens all the time to couples. He is afraid of not having sex all the time, and she is afraid of having sex all the time. Really, it is no big deal whether you have sex all the time or not. We make it into a big deal, but it is not. We struggle with it like there are only two options—either have sex all the time, which frightens her, or do not have sex all the time, which frightens him. You can always tell when the ego is plugged in, because it looks like there are only one or two options and not a solution that would satisfy everybody.

When you are in your big mind, you can see that there are a few hundred things you could be doing about sex that do not occur to your egos because you are plugged into the world of fear. You are living in the universe of fear about sex—both of you. And when you forgive each other, you can shift to the universe of love, full of possibilities—lots of sex, no sex at all, just holding hands, just fantasizing about it, fantasizing your greatest fears, acting them out with each other, on and on—all these other possibilities that are very expansive. Right now you two are contracted about it. You are a couple of sex fiends. You think about it a lot. It is always on your minds. And it is a big deal. And when you have your breakthroughs about it, the sex will be better than ever. I appreciate your openness with us.

Q. Thank you.

A. Any other questions?

Q. When we talk about our parents, what if you have only good feelings about your parents and felt they loved you and they are gone—they have died? I do not seem to have anything to forgive in my parents.

A. That is great! Do you have a relatively effortless love-filled existence? Now, do not worry about bragging about it, but just in a very humble way, do you have an effortless love-filled existence?

Q. Not particularly...

A. I asked because if your parents are as you described, there is no reason for you not to be happy. When your parents are real loving, what happens is that you just go around loving everybody, feeling lots of gratitude for life, and seeing the magnificence in other people. It is a lot easier to appreciate people than to criticize them. That is what life is about. But, also, sometimes people have a special loving relationship with their parents and they get a little arrogant about it and will not allow others into the club. That is sad, because it is taking everything they gave you and distorting it.

I do not know what in particular is going on with you. Maybe all you need to do is start being more loving with people. Maybe you are shy. Maybe you were an only child. It does not matter what the reasons are. All you need to do to make your life with us earthlings (because we are your family, you know) happier like your family of origin, is to be more open and loving with us.

If you had really loving parents who were acknowledging, affectionate, nourishing, supportive, who encouraged you to go out in the world, then you ought to be having a great life. If they were really loving, but acted like the world is a scary place, taught you not to take too many chances out there, then you just need to forgive them for that. Then start practising reaching out.

Q. It seems so foreign?

A. You can always tell when you are on the verge of stepping into a part of the forest that you have not been into before, because when you are right out there, your ego starts screaming, "It's dangerous! Something awful is going to happen!" You just need to notice that is what your ego is doing, take a deep breath, take another step, and go farther.

Q. Some people just do not seem worth it.

A. All I can say is that there are no exceptions to this wisdom. The ego can always think of very gripping and very provocative circumstances where it would not work, but there are no exceptions. There is nobody you cannot practice this on if you are willing and it will transform the quality of your life if you are willing to practice it.

Q. What about phobias? Extreme fears?

A. Usually phobias are symbolic. They represent something you do not want to face. Actually, they represent a solution to a problem even scarier than the phobia itself. So you have the fear of heights or being closed in or whatever...and you handle this fear in this dysfunctional way, because it is a solution to a problem somewhere else that you do not even want to look at or come close to. That is one useful perspective on phobias.

Another thing about phobias reminds me of what Freud said, "Behind the fear, the wish..." If you are really afraid of something, there is another part of you that is very attracted to it. And if you explore that attraction, you sometimes discover some really interesting things about yourself. Phobias are fascinating and there are all kinds of interesting stories about phobias that I will skip for now. You could probably tell us a few yourself.

Q. How do you forgive Hitler? Or anybody who perpetrated some really horrible thing?

A. You forgive them just like you forgive anyone else. You recognize that their bizarre destructive behavior was a twisted request for love and underneath that fearful behavior they are your brother and in some way—I know this sounds impossible to believe—underneath that fearful behavior they have a love for you and a desire for the best for you. Even if...even if they were trying to kill you. One friend of mine was being whipped by a Nazi. He just looked at the man, said, "I love you," and the whiplashes on his back started fading right then. The Nazi dropped his whip and stopped beating him.

There are no exceptions to this wisdom. There is nobody beyond forgiveness. Now for a Hitler, the most loving thing you can do is stop him—or any mass murderer. I mean, talk about addictive compulsive behavior: The man was tortured. He was not happy behaving that way.

Now, the ego thinks that your righteous indignation makes you more powerful. But, if you come from love and forgiveness, you are fifty times more powerful. If you want to "make a difference" in any situation that is unfolding in the world—hunger, for instance, your state of mind is a significant factor. If you are judgmental towards the Ethiopian government because it keeps trucks with food from reaching the starving people, the kind of energy you put out in your state of judgment contributes to the problem.   It actually makes it more difficult to redistribute the food. If you approach the problem from a loving, forgiving standpoint, like the army is made up of your brothers—and underneath their fearful behavior they want the best for you and their starving countrymen, it is much more effective. In fact, miracles take place when people come from this loving, forgiving space. I mean, armies behave in ways that nobody would have predicted when you are in a loving space. But...it does not work as a technique. It only works as a surrender of the heart.

Q. What if you don't feel like forgiving? Do you fake it until you make it? Do you force yourself to say forgiving things?

A. Sometimes you can do that. Say you are driving down the freeway and somebody cuts right in front of you. You think, "That jerk! I wish I had my tank. I would flatten him..." And then you think, "Now, wait a minute—I remember what Leonard said Friday night. Okay, I forgive you for your ignorant behavior towards me..." Sometimes when you say that statement out loud you still want to flatten them,...but sometimes you have this amazing experience. You feel this softening take place inside your body. It is a wonderful feeling, and all of a sudden you are thinking, "Gee, maybe one of the guy's kids got hurt. I hope he gets home safely." So, you are actually hurrying him on his way and wishing the traffic would part for him. A moment ago you wanted to murder the guy. So it does have a transformational quality when you just force yourself to say it even when you do not feel like it.

On the other hand, if you say something like, "Well, all right, I forgive Hitler for his ignorant, fearful behavior towards the planet," and you say it but you just do not feel it and it is not really there...well, then you need to say, "I refuse to forgive Hitler for his ignorant behavior towards the planet even though it brings out the Hitler in me." or, "I refuse to forgive _____ (mom, dad, boss, etc.) for their ignorant behavior towards me, in spite of the cost."

And you just own that. You just own it without beating yourself up like "that is who I am for this moment right here and now." It opens up the space for you to come a little closer to Hitler as your brother...underneath all that drama, the horror, the ugliness, the genocide, and all...you see, there is a little Hitler in all of us and we do not want to face it. We want to say Hitler was the bad one. He is awful. He is over there and all us good guys are over here. When you do that, you weaken yourself. When you refuse to acknowledge the Hitler inside you or even the possibility he is there, you weaken yourself and you actually put out a kind of energy that fertilizes the possibility of another Hitler appearing. Whereas by forgiving him and connecting to him as your lost brother, you decrease the chance of another Hitler appearing. You learn to love the Hitler inside you that you have refused to love for your whole life. You see, to deny that

Hitler inside you makes you much more able to commit a terrible act against humanity. By the way, the only time in all of my seminars or groups that we ever came close to a fight was when a pacifist was about to get into it with somebody because he so strongly objected to the man's behavior. It is that denial of the Hitler inside you that can lead to violence. Or look at all the murders committed under the guise of religion.

Q. I feel that I have forgiven. Can I speak of the inappropriate behavior of the person involved?

A. If you truly have forgiven the person and they are acting like a jerk, then you can, coming from a real loving space, tell them that they are acting like a jerk. On the other hand, if you are doing this con-job on yourself and trying to be this slick, loving, enlightened person who is trying to get them to change or to "see the light," then, in a rather sophisticated way, you are still judging them.

You can say exactly the same words coming from love or coming from fear—exactly the same words—and if you are truly loving and forgiving the person, you will be amazed at what you can get away with saying. But if you are trying to fix them and change them, you are adding more poison to the situation.

You can usually tell the difference as you are confronting the person with their behavior, because if you are truly forgiving them, then what you feel is love, like, "Listen, I just need to give you this feedback to be the best friend I possibly can be. You were acting like a jerk just now. What you do with this information is up to you. I am not going to withhold my love until you change, or expect you to act differently. I am just being the best friend I can be, by pointing this out to you. What you do with it is up to you." That is the kind of feedback you give when you are coming from a really loving space. If you give this feedback and you have this hidden agenda in the back of your mind that they ought to change, then you are not coming from love and forgiveness.

Q. I am coming from a much larger perspective. I have been learning and respecting feminist analysis and thought, and I hear over and over feminists say, "Anger unites us." It is a contrasted feeling, but it is right...

A. Well, okay, anger is one step above apathy or submission, but it is not a very high state of consciousness. And women who are in that space will never truly be free until they forgive their ignorant brothers and connect to them as brothers. They will never reach their ultimate state of personal power and peace of mind as long as they are still making their brothers wrong (judging). So anger is better than submitting and swallowing all that garbage that men put out all those years, but it is definitely not the highest, most powerful, most liberating state of consciousness. The ultimate freedom will come from forgiving our brothers and feeling connected with them—feeling a peaceful connection with them and feeling an appreciation for everything our brothers gave us. But when you are busy making your brothers wrong, you are stuck. It is okay, if it is just a stage you go through, but if you never get out of it, it is sad and limiting.

Q. Would you say the same applies to Blacks?

A. Absolutely. Look at Gandhi. He brought the British Empire to its knees with this wisdom...

Q. Can you elaborate on that? I would like to hear you talk about acts of intervention against violent acts, or against potentially planet-killing acts. Take nuclear arms, for instance. What about stopping people, not talking to groups in power, but stopping them?

A. Okay, let us take the nuclear arms race. You want to intervene in the nuclear arms race. And you are making Reagan and Gorbachev wrong. You are not going to be nearly as effective as when you forgive them for their ignorant behavior and you recognize them as your brothers. Whatever you want to do—gather signatures on a petition, write them letters, walk to some place, take a stand somewhere or whatever, you will be much more effective if you realize that we are all brothers and sisters, are all in this together—not in an intellectual way, but in your heart. You need to surrender to Gorbachev and Reagan in terms of **underneath their fearful behavior they love you**, they want the best for you, and they are your brothers. They might be out to lunch, but they are still your brothers.

Q. I don't have trouble with that, but what about some person who is doing something to cause grave injury. What do you do to prevent it from happening?

A. You have to use your intuition or instincts. You may not be the one to stop them. If you want to stop them, you need to make your intervention in a loving way, even if you shout at the top of your lungs, and, they might commit violence anyway. You have to do all this very humbly, and you may need to surrender your own impotence in the situation.

If you walk around the corner and someone is being mugged, there is no pat technique. You have to take each situation intuitively and do what feels right to you. You might just stop in your tracks and start sending love to the mugger and muggee. You do not know what you are going to do in advance. There are some really interesting examples of what people have done. A woman is working in this little market late at night and this kid comes in and pulls a gun on her and says, "give me your money." And the woman says, "How much do you need, son?"

and the kid starts crying.... Another woman is on the subway late at night in New York and these four guys get on and they look at her and start talking about how easy it would be to rape her. Just in her head, she starts sending them love. Pretty soon they stop talking about raping her and then a stop or two later they get off. One kid hops back on, says, "Have a good day," and hops off... That is quite a shift in behavior.

We like to think, "If that happens to me, I will just do such and such..." You do not know what you will do. You might just sit there and wet your pants. But, in general, the more you practice love and forgiveness, the more effortless and love-filled your life becomes. It does not matter if you are working on starving children in Africa, the nuclear arms race, racial conflicts, violence in the cities, or whatever.

There was a group of meditators in Atlanta that went to the most violent part of Atlanta and meditated in the evening for two or three weeks in a row. The rate of violence dropped significantly when they meditated and for two weeks after. They did it again weeks later and the rate dropped, but not as much. I think that the second time they did it, they had expectations that got in their way. The first time was a wide open experiment: "Let's do this and see what happens..."

So what does all this mean? It means that all of our minds are connected in a way that is beyond understanding. It means that when we dwell on judgments and negativity, we make it easier for people to do destructive things. It means that when we dwell on loving thoughts, we make it easier for people to do loving things.

❤ The Stance of Peace and Power

So here is the stance of peace and power. With your hands open and your palms turned up. This is the mind/body/ spirit stance for maximum love and abundance and beauty to flow through your life. But the ego hates this stance. The ego wants to either push away love and abundance and say, "It won't happen," "I don't deserve it" or grab on and squeeze and say, "Oh, I've got to have it," "Let's make it happen," or "I can't live without it." But hands open, palms up is the maximum stance for personal power and peace of mind. And, if you practice this, the more you practice, the easier it gets and the more your intuition tells you what to do about a mugging, a riot, the arms race, conflict between the sexes—all of that.

Q. I know what you are saying and I imagine that it is the ego that finds stories like what happened to Jesus Christ or that social worker who was loving and giving and found herself trussed and beaten and raped... This is the kind of thing the ego keeps alive.

A. Oh, absolutely!

Q. And regarding your vulnerability, do you just offer your life up for love?

A. That is right. You offer your life up for love because it is the main reason you are here on the planet. Love is all there is. The rest we make up. Now it is true that some people practice this wisdom in a masochistic way and do not realize they are doing it. And some practice this wisdom in a selfish, manipulating way and are fooling themselves.

Remember: When you hear this wisdom, your big mind or

higher self wants to surrender to it and your ego or little mind wants to polish up your rackets with it.

In a very profound way, that social worker and her attackers are brothers and sister. That is the bottom line, no matter how horrible the particular event is. Our ego loves to think of these examples: "Well, how could you possibly apply it to this horrible experience?" But we learn and grow from these terrible experiences. Or, we can use them to reinforce our fears and barriers. Gandhi forgave the man who shot him. The Pope forgave the man who shot him. Living this wisdom is the most powerful, effortless way to live.

Q. I am interested in what happens when we are grieving. It is like we have a lot of pain involved with the loss of love and then a fear of going ahead and we get stuck there...

A. You are absolutely right.

Q. ...and it almost seems forgiveness is something else above love and fear.

A. And when you get stuck in grieving, it is usually the only way the ego can hang onto whatever you lost. Grieving is a natural process. You lose something or someone and you go through a mourning process. You cry, feel the loss, and then you forgive the person for dying and leaving or abandoning you. If it is a deep loss, you may even need to go back and forgive your mother for leaving you when you were five, or whatever, because the loss triggers the experience of "early similars." That is one of the advantages regarding something that plugs you in that deeply: It is a chance to heal from the initial pain and/or similar events in the past.

If you are stuck in grieving, it is usually the ego hanging on because when you really let go (of this person or event or house or job or whatever it is you lost) you do not know who you will be without it. Your identity is so tied up in who or what was lost that you have no idea who you will be if you truly let go. You do not want to find out. You are too scared.

If you are willing to find out, you have a brand new life and that is very wonderful. Forgiveness is the healing tool that allows you to move on with your life. If you practice it enough, you get to a place where you hardly even need it anymore.

Q. Can you work with the body and forgiveness? It seems like the body's pain is what is uncontrollable. It just comes.

A. Pain and trauma are stored in the body. If you can sob or tremble, it is an important part of healing. The body is releasing stored up pain or trauma.

I usually encourage people to breathe and surrender and just cry...just cry and cry and cry. You are afraid you will cry for two hours—or a half a day or longer. But if you really surrender to your tears, it heals you and prepares you to move on. Another way people get stuck in mourning and loss is to resist or fight their tears. They never allow themselves to go deeply enough into the pain and trauma to really cleanse it from their body. Anything else you want to say or ask about that?

Q. Well, it just seems to take time.... Two hours is fine, but then maybe I go for a week or two weeks and it keeps on coming...and I keep going through it and...it is getting tedious. I guess I am getting tired of it.

A. Well, if it has been going on for a long time, you may be hanging onto the loss. Or it could mean that there is some loss from your childhood you have not dealt with and you need to face that. Face that and surrender to it and forgive whoever left you or whoever took whatever you wanted away from you in early childhood. Let go of that one and forgive the people involved. It may not take that long unless it involves death. If you are inordinately attached to your body and you really think you are your body, then   you may get hung up on death. But you are not your body. It is an interesting part of you, but it is not the most basic part. There is something more significant to you than your body and we do not have a lot of understanding of what that is. We get glimpses of it. Birth and death are two of the most interesting parts of life and they are transitions, but you are not your body.

Q. What do you do with professional burnout? I have been a counselor and therapist for two to three years and I keep coming up to the fact I still have stuff to deal with. I go really hard for six months or so and then I collapse. Then I go again and then I collapse again. I am thinking of going back into the social services, but I get so frustrated—not with people like Gorbachev or Reagan, but people in lesser positions of power. I try to love them and forgive them until the cows come home, and nothing happens and that really devastates me.

A. I have been doing mental health work for twenty-five years and I love it more today than ever. I am really grateful for that. I think a lot of it is because I love my work. I do the best I possibly can for people and what they do with it is their responsibility. So, some things that transform mental health burnout are:

1. committing yourself to your clients and doing the best you can for them,

2. committing yourself to your administrators and making the best suggestions you can without coming from judgment and making them wrong, and

3. being grateful for your job. If you practice all that lovingly, if you are really committed to clients and agency and whoever pays your salary (the government if you are on government payroll) and you really give them your best, then something will start to shift. Either you will let go of a lot of stress or you will just go in there, do the best you can, and what they do with it is their business. You will go home and know you did the best you could do. I look at money as a miracle that allows us to pass around our love and energy. When I pay taxes, I am giving my love and energy. My taxes pay salaries in social services. Those workers are passing my love and energy on to people who need it. If you view your work as passing out the love of thousands of taxpayers, you might enjoy yourself more. (Of course, it is also a channel for expressing your love.)

When people walk out my door, I try to make sure I have given them my very best. This scares my ego because it does not want me to say certain things. Sometimes I feel like I have really gone out on a limb and my ego fears looking foolish. Some of this wisdom is beyond logic. I have had experiences where I felt compelled to share this wisdom out of my commitment to people and my ego felt very uncomfortable afterwards. But I may get a card five days later from the man's wife telling me, "So many people have tried to tell him what you told him and he just wouldn't listen to anyone else. But he really heard you. I will always be grateful for that session."

Q. I guess my expectations are too high. My ego wants to see change...for the other person.

A. So, when you work with your clients, is it okay that they do not make use of you...turn their back on what you have to offer? Are you willing to be impotent with your clients? Because that is where a lot of the stress can come from. You have to be there and give them your best and be willing to be impotent. In fact,

41

until you are willing to be impotent, there are going to be some real difficult times coming your way. Clients will show up that will rub your nose in it until you get it. Remember, your clients are your teachers. On one level, you are supposed to help them and you do your best to do that. On another level, be open to the possibility that they are there to teach you. We teach what we need to learn. When you surrender to your own impotence, much of your clients' resistance may melt away.

Another thing is that if I had more than twenty sessions a week with my individuals, couples, and families, I do not know if I would love my work as much as I do. Diet and exercise are important, too, in stress reduction. If you are not taking really brisk walks three times a week or swimming or doing some exercise you love (for me it is basketball), and eating a lot of raw fruits and vegetables and staying away from caffeine, alcohol, white sugar, and white flour, you will be much more susceptible to stress. You do not have to be rigid about it, but certain things make you much more vulnerable on the roller coaster of life. A small glass of wine with dinner or a beer is not that big of a deal, but people are into caffeine or alcohol or sugar in ways that make them more vulnerable to stress. And if you do not exercise, you are more prone to depression. So, those are some of the stress factors involved. (I also lift weights and jog or race walk several times per week.)

Q. You said that this way of being, this way of focusing, is effortless, more effortless than anything else. That is not my experience: I find I constantly have to struggle to get back to the headspace or whatever you want to call it...

A. Heartspace.

Q. Heartspace—yes—and a lot of the time I am not there. What I want to know is are you in this space all the

time?

A. No-o-o-o (laughter)...but what I have found is the more you practice it, the easier it gets. In the beginning, you really need to work at it. There was a fork in the road and you are three steps down in the universe of fear before you realize that there was even a fork in the road. You have to take a slow deep breath and ask yourself, "What is going on here? I feel so angry and judgmental! Who haven't I forgiven? What am I afraid of?" You just have to back up and take a stand for love and forgiveness. It does require discipline and concentration at first—not for everybody. For some people it is easier than for others, but the more you practice it, the easier it gets. And you do get to a place where it is relatively easy most of the time. I would say that it is relatively easy for me most of the time, but I am liable to be really upset tomorrow or act like a complete fool. You just have to stay humble about it. I am very grateful for my life the way it is now. I have never felt so relaxed about money, love, sex, my body, etc. I love and appreciate my wife, kids, friends, and clients tremendously. Sometimes when I forget to trim a nail and tear   it on the basketball court, or get one of my toes stepped on out there and it starts to turn black and blue for the tenth time in thirty years of playing, why, I get a little depressed. But, really, my life is easier than ever and I expect it will just get easier and easier. But I also get upset sometimes or get scared. I find the more I tell the truth, the less I stay in any one space. Remember, it is usually most difficult to practice love and forgiveness with your parents, children, and mate. Your little mind wants to repeat again and again, with your mate, all your unfinished business that you have with your parents.

Q. Do you ever get angry?

A. Yes, I get angry and judgmental. Not only that, but as a mental health person and professional saint, (laughter) I try never to do anything that hurts anybody else or poisons them and try never to be judgmental. Sometimes I am judgmental and cover it up and do not even notice I am doing it. It is an occupational hazard that goes with being a therapist and always trying to be a good person. That is one of my coping mechanisms. So sometimes I am acting nice because I am afraid and I do not even know I am acting like a jerk. Other times I am acting nice because I really am a very easy going, loving, gentle person. But certainly, I make mistakes. Sometimes when I see someone being mean to a child, it is hard for me to say, "They are just afraid. It is just a twisted request for love." Sometimes I just get righteous about it. Then I recognize that my righteousness is actually going to make things worse, going to make them treat the child worse, because the kind of energy you put out when you are into judgment is toxic and it tends to bring out the worst in people. When you are in the universe of love and forgiveness, the kind of energy you put out tends to bring out the best in people.

Further questions by a woman who heard me on a radio talk show.

November 26, 1988

Dear Mr. Shaw:

I have heard you on the Patrick Conlon CFRB radio show. Would you kindly advise which of your books or work would help me.

I am 67 years old, my sister 62, and my brother 60, and there is no nice relationship between us.

My sister lives in Germany. She closed the door on us for a visit. She wants us there, to live with her. She enlarged our little home to accommodate my brother with his 20 years younger wife (Romanian) and two sons (13 and 11) , and myself, in spite of our warnings years ago that we are not returning on our retirement to live back home.

Also, my brother is an alcoholic and nothing can change him, not even two major heart operations within last 20 years. Two months ago, he too closed the door on me, because I told him that it is very painful to look at his destruction and hidden bottles.

I am Catholic and try to go to church daily. It is true that I get help from the mass but I would like to be a lot happier than I am. I am praying for my brother and my sister for the last 25 years for the above reasons.

I would appreciate your response.

I wish you a nice Christmas and a happy New Year!

Yours truly,

Renate

Dear Renate:

My wife and I were very touched by your letter. The key to your freedom and happiness lies in the fact that you feel better when you pray for your brother and sister.

There is another type of prayer or meditation that will help you feel even better, but I need to explain something to you first. Your brother and sister are caught in the universe of fear. His drinking and her shutting you out are the ways that they handle their fear. I get the feeling that they are both addicted to their fearful responses and it would be wise and liberating if you did not expect them to change. You can pray for their healing and, even more important, you can picture them or *visualize them as already healed* and sending you a tremendous amount of love. But it is most important that you do not judge them for their fearful behavior and do not expect them to change. But I guarantee you that under their fear, they love you tremendously.

Stay away from your brother when he drinks, but in your mind send him love and forgiveness. It is very important that you not judge him for drinking. In fact, anytime you have a negative thought about your brother or sister, just notice that you had a negative thought, gently set it aside, and replace it with a loving, forgiving thought.

Now, Renate, comes something very important. Buried deeply underneath the fears of your brother and sister, they actually love you very much and want the very best for you, *(even if they are not consciously aware of it!).* Meditating on this deep love that they have for you will help you tremendously towards your goal of happiness.

In fact, you might find yourself smiling or crying right now as you read this (kind of like the feeling of "coming home"). You see, deep down underneath your fear, you already know everything I am telling you.

It also would help you to visualize or picture you, your brother, and your sister all sitting peacefully in Germany, bathing in each other's love, like people bathe in the sun. Be open to the possibility that this could actually happen, but do not expect it to happen.

I am sending you several articles and a cassette tape to support this wisdom. I have written most of them, but one particularly useful piece I did not write. I want you to study it. It is a list of "do's and don't's" for being close to an alcoholic.

Love and peace,

Leonard Shaw

❤ SELF HEALING EXERCISES

"So it is that we must weather that dark time,
the period of transformation when what is
familiar has been taken away and the new
richness is not yet ours." —Ram Dass

Are you ready to proceed with your self healing? This pathway is not fair. Are you ready to give up your pre-occupation with what is fair? You do not have to forgive everyone right now. You do not have to like what we are doing or are about to do. You do not even have to believe in what we are doing, you just have to practice it. There is no substitute for courage and action! You **do** need a desire for happiness, peace, and power. Not power over other people, but power over how you experience people, events, and life. You do not have to want to forgive people, but you do need to **want to get to where** you want to forgive people.

So here comes a significant sentence. "I forgive my parents and others for their ignorant behavior towards me."

Say it out loud or whisper it inside your head. Can you relax as you say it and let it bathe over you, or does your body tighten up?

By "ignorant behavior," I mean that **all** negative behavior comes from fear. If someone behaved in a mean or destructive way towards you, it means that they were (and maybe still are) caught up in the universe of fear. They were listening to (or indulging) their ego or "little mind," but underneath that fearful behavior, they love you and want the best for you ***even if they are not consciously aware of it***.

So, by forgiving people for their ignorant behavior towards you, you are opening your heart and your mind to a deep loving connection that we all have with each other. Remember though, you do not have to hang around people you forgive. Some of them are still caught in the universe of fear and they are not much fun to be around. In your minds, bathe them in love and forgiveness and stay away from them. Or visit them while they are positive (or sober, for example, if they are alcoholic) and walk away from them when they get negative (or start drinking). My next statement is important. As you walk away, repeat over and over in your head, "I love you, I forgive you, I bless you, I release you, I love you, I forgive you, I bless you, I release you."

What your ego or little mind wants to do as you walk away is judge the person for being negative or drinking or attacking you (or whatever their negative behavior is). If you listen to your ego, you will poison yourself. You need to be able to love and forgive people as you walk away from them. (Instead of enumerating all that is wrong with them.)

So if you can relax and breathe deeply as you say, "I forgive my parents and others for their ignorant behavior towards me," that is a very good sign. You are ready to proceed with harvesting and claiming some of the many benefits of the painful or traumatic events of your life. (Remember, every negative experience is always at least as positive as it is negative if we can just open ourselves up to it.) If you tighten up with the "I forgive..." sentence, or get strong images of people you just cannot or will not forgive, then you may need to express some negativity of your own to "clear the decks" for forgiveness.

❤ CLEARING THE DECKS

Regarding the person with whom you are still angry and/or do not want to forgive, you need to write them an angry, nasty letter. It usually helps to exaggerate your anger and name calling. (It matters not if the person is dead or alive or if you know their whereabouts.) Remember, this is only for people whom you are unable to forgive and you must make it a very angry, blameful letter or you will not be able to move closer to forgiveness.

Once you have your nasty letter completed (be sure to sign it), put it in your sock or underwear drawer. (***Do not*** mail it and ***do not*** give it to the person at whom you are angry.) Tell yourself, "There is all my garbage and poison with (***dad or whomever***). I know right where it is if I need it. I do not have to carry it around inside me anymore." Your ego or little mind actually thinks that hanging onto that garbage protects you from future pain. The fact is that hanging onto that garbage is like a magnet. It attracts other people's garbage into your life, and usually involves people whose dynamics are similar to the person with whom you are unfinished or unhealed!

Next, take another sheet of paper and draw a line down the middle. On the left side of the paper, write, "I refuse to forgive (their name) for their ignorant behavior towards me, in spite of the cost." Immediately then on the right side of the page, you write the very first thing that pops into your head. Repeat this five times. It looks something like this:

I refuse to forgive my father for his ignorant behavior towards me in spite of the cost.

Nothing! This is a stupid exercise. Leonard doesn't know what he's talking about.

I refuse to forgive my father for his ignorant behavior towards me in spite of the cost.

I see my father working on farms around British Columbia. He is ten years old.

I refuse to forgive my father for his ignorant behavior towards me in spite of the cost.

It's a wonder my father turned out to be as loving as he was.

I refuse to forgive my father for his ignorant behavior towards me in spite of the cost.

Back to blah. I'm afraid my hurt is buried so deep I'll never find it.

I refuse to forgive my father for his ignorant behavior towards me in spite of the cost.

I just want him to put his arms around me and tell me he's proud of me.

Now, on the left side of a page, write, "I forgive my father (or whomever) for his ignorant behavior towards me." And on the right side write the first thing that pops into your head or heart. Repeat this ten times. It helps to write fast and not think or analyze what you are doing.

I forgive my father for his
ignorant behavior towards me.

Yes, I do. Yes, I do. Yes,
I do.—a strange feeling—
I feel foolish and exposed.

I forgive my father for his
ignorant behavior towards me.

My penmanship is terrible.

I forgive my father for his
ignorant behavior towards me.

My dad only had two years
of schooling. I wish I could
have been his father and
given him all the love he
deserved.

I forgive my father for his
ignorant behavior towards me.

Actually, all I really need
to do is be my own good
father and give myself all
the love I deserve.

I forgive my father for his
ignorant behavior towards me.

I feel close to my father.
I'm glad we were so loving
and affectionate with each
other those last two weeks
before he died.

I forgive my father for his
ignorant behavior towards me.

I feel peaceful—content—
and like improving my
handwriting.

I forgive my father for his
ignorant behavior towards me.

I like writing clearly. I
wish I had beautiful
handwriting.

I forgive my father for his
ignorant behavior towards me.

I'm sitting up now, trying
for a better posture.

I forgive my father for his
ignorant behavior towards me.

I want a miracle with my
handwriting.

I forgive my father for his ignorant behavior towards me.	This could take a long time and a lot of work, but my friends would find it much easier to read my letters (ha, ha, smile, smile)

You can repeat this process (i.e., 5 "I refuse..." and 10 "I forgive...") several times at one sitting or several times in a week. It works differently for different people. And remember, there is no substitute for **courage and action**!

❤ THE THANK YOU LETTER

Is it okay with you if people who have hurt you a lot make a significant contribution to your life? You may get tired of these questions or feel I get repetitious, but these are very important questions. You have no idea how strongly attached your ego is to hurts from the past! If you ever get an **honest** glimpse at this attraction, you will be quite humbled by the experience. Your ego decides that someone has done something awful to you and refuses to be open to the possibility that something good will come of it. Something good will always come of it if we just open our mind and heart and let it happen.

For many people, the big issue or barrier is how they feel wronged by their parents. Therefore these people lose much of their personal power and groundedness (feeling solid psychologically, emotionally, and physically planted here on earth) in their unhealed, negative feelings around their parents. If you have done quite a bit of the forgiveness work described earlier and want to move farther into personal power and peace of mind, you may be ready for the "Thank You Letter."

The "Thank You Letter" is more than it seems. On the surface it looks like a nice thing to do for the person you thank. (It is.) But what it does for you is far greater than what it does for the person being thanked. In some ways, it is beyond explanation. It has to do with the paradox that "To give is to receive." (I am still learning about that one.)

The other dynamic this letter relates to is what I call "owning your roots." As we grow up, we often go through a stage where we disown our parents to some degree. Some people get stuck there and it cripples them for life. Others re-connect with their parents quite harmoniously, but still do not fully own the gifts they received from their parents. You become a much more powerful and peaceful person when you acknowledge people for their contributions to your life and this is particularly true with your parents. Even a biological parent you have never met can be thanked for your life and the genetic gifts you received from them.

Also, the more you evolve in your growth, the more grateful you become. The letter I wrote to my Dad as I was writing this book has many more "thanks for gifts" in it than the thank you letters I wrote him two or three years ago. (He died the Spring of 1987.)

Make a list of all the gifts your parents gave you. Not presents (unless it was a particularly special present) but experiences, lessons, special moments, behaviors they modeled, your genetics, habits, places they took you, things they showed you, etc. Usually it works best if you do your parents one at a time. From that list, construct a "Thank You Letter."

Dear Dad:
Recently I have been thinking about all the ways in which you

have contributed to my life and I am writing to tell you about it. There is really a lot more, but I hope this letter gives you some idea of how I feel.

• You showed me how to be thoughtful, attentive and take good care of my lady. You love babies, I just know you played with me and talked to me a lot when I was a baby.

• You are very intelligent, I inherited good smarts from you.

• You were clever at fixing many things. I will always remember the time we fixed the broken water pipes in 1 or 2 feet of snow.

• I have good coordination and reflexes. I am a very attentive and good driver and I thank you for these things.

• On those 6 Sundays a year the store was closed, you and mom would always try to take us someplace special like the ocean, the Rain Forest, Hurricane Ridge or Lake Quinault.

• You always had an interesting way of looking at people or life or nature with depth and insight (if I would just listen).

• There are 3 simple things that I value highly, admire you for, and try to emulate. You were always honest, hard working (I call it committed or giving your best) and treated people fairly (though I did not always feel you treated me fairly (smile)).

• You had a good sense of humor and liked to play and laugh.

• You always took good care of your clothes and dressed tastefully.

• You always took good care of your car, belongings, tools, etc.

• You were clean and neat but not obsessive.

• You had inner strengths and standards that you let no one infringe upon.

• You were quiet but never afraid to speak out and earned the respect and admiration of people wherever you settled.

• You have good rhythm and encouraged me to play drums, a source of much joy.

• You are a very charitable person and have done much to make the world a better place.

• You spend money freely but not foolishly and you can also save money.

All of the above have been great gifts to me directly and indirectly and I thank you from the bottom of my heart.

Love and thanks,

Son

If you have not done this before, it is often easier to start with a list that you later turn into a letter.

❤ REPROGRAMMING TAPE

When we are born, we start making conclusions and decisions about what life and people will be like for us. "Life is easy." "Life is a struggle." "People are wonderful and safe." "People are painful and dangerous." "If you show your real feelings, it will be used against you." Once we make these decisions, we look for evidence to support them and ignore evidence that contradicts them. Your "little mind" would rather be right than happy, regarding these decisions, but we usually do not take responsibility for this "life stance." You see, usually these decisions are negative and really limit what is possible in our future. We are constantly creating our ***experience of life*** while thinking ***life is happening to us*** or someone is doing it to us. As Dr. Jerry Jampolsky says in his *Mini Course for Healing Relationships*, "We really cannot change the world we live in or other people. We ***can*** change how we perceive the world, how we perceive others, and how we perceive ourselves."

Here is a powerful exercise for reprogramming these old decisions or "tapes" that have been running your life.

Please do not bother with this exercise unless you are ready for a significant change in your life. It is a waste of time if you are not willing for something new, different, and beautiful to show up in your life. Paradoxically, remember, it is still the most powerful stance if you are also willing to have a meaningless experience with this exercise.

So pick an area of your life that you would like to transform. (i.e., relationships with the opposite sex, money, food, sex, career, art, music). Take a sheet of paper and draw a line down the middle. (You may need 3 or 4 sheets.) Let us say you chose relationships. On the left side, write all your painful, scary, disappointing experiences with relationships or with the opposite sex. You do not need to strain for every single experience. Just trust that, what is useful, will come to mind in this process. Also, be open to the possibility that something quite traumatic (totally forgotten) may surface. If you start crying, just breathe deeply and completely surrender to your tears. It is a wonderful opportunity to start your healing. Whatever painful experience comes to mind in this process, go ahead and write it on the left side of the paper even if it seems not to apply to your focus. Some may be directly painful (i.e., your third grade teacher embarrassed you in front of the class or one of your parents picked on you and never told you they loved you). Some may be indirectly painful (i.e., your parents were mean to each other or unfaithful). Some may be isolated, one-time events and some may have been chronic or repetitive.

When you have finished your list, hold it in your hand and ask yourself, "Am I ready for every painful item on this list to actually become a source of peace, power, richness, beauty, and strength in my life?" Do not worry about how we will accomplish this, just look in your heart and see if you are willing for it to happen.

If you are willing, then on the right side of the page, next to each painful incident, write an affirmation related to the incident. Affirmations are short positive statements like, "Underneath her fearful behavior, my mother loves me very much." If you are willing, you can find an affirmation around any painful or traumatic event. Let us look at a true extreme example. A father would regularly take his daughter, in the middle of the night, to the basement. He would tie her, rape her, untie her and leave. All without talking to her and he would speak little to her during the day time. He was a very frightened bully. (All bullies are.) He hated himself for his behavior and projected his hatred onto his family (four people). If we could peel back all his layers of fear, we would discover that it broke his heart to abuse his daughter and that underneath his fear, he loved her and wanted the best for her.

When I did some healing therapy with this woman, she ended up with a peaceful feeling about her father that gave her a fresh start in life, and with men.

So even in extreme cases you can still create an affirmation of "Underneath his fearful behavior, my father loves me and wants the best for me." Another affirmation you can often use for extreme events is, "I have a deep sensitivity to (or compassion for) other people's pain."

Sometimes a painful experience turns into two affirmations. When I was small, my father made me eat everything on my plate and I hated peas and egg yolks. "My father made me eat peas and egg yolks" turned into 1. "I eat what I want and it nourishes me," and 2. "My father loves me very much."

If you are doing this process and you have some painful events for which you cannot create an affirmation, just send them to me along with a stamped, self-addressed envelope (Leonard Shaw, 702 - 11th East., Seattle, WA 98102), and I will send you back appropriate affirmations. I have never met a traumatic event about which I could not find an affirmation.

Affirmations must be positive statements. "Women are no longer mean to me" is not an affirmation. All your unconscious hears is "Women are mean to me." Change it to "Women love being good to me." For further tips and information on affirmations, see my article in the appendix entitled, "How to Make Room for More Money to Show Up in Your Life."

The next step in this powerful process is to dictate onto an audio cassette, each of these affirmations three times in a row. (Do not dictate the negative side of the page.) It is important to do it with **conviction** and **vitality** even if you must pretend you are an actor. Pretend you feel conviction and vitality even if you do not. Sometimes it helps to emphasize a different word each time:

My **father** loves me very much.
My father **loves** me very much.
My father loves me **very** much.

This may sound like a lot, but most people end up with a tape that is only five to ten minutes long.

Now comes the most powerful part of the process. Listen to your tape **at least three times a day** for two months. (In your car, while dressing or eating breakfast, while going to sleep at night, while meditating, while exercizing or jogging.) When I did this process I listened to mine ten times a day. Listening I often had a slightly strange feeling (a little scary, a little exciting) like a subtle significant change was taking place on several levels. In a positive way I felt I would never quite be the same.

It helps to get a short tape and fill both sides with your affirmations. That way you are not required to stop the tape, reverse it, and start over. Here is an example from a woman who had fears and negative tapes in her head about being a success (even though her work was selling in galleries coast to coast.)

I will never make a good living doing my artwork.	I ~~can~~ make a good income with ease doing my art work.
No one takes me seriously	People love me and appreciate who I am.
I'm too neurotic to make things work smoothly.	I have a good business sense and ~~can~~ work with ease.
If I'm a success I'm boring.	Successful people are inspirational. My success is an exciting inspiration to others.
If I'm a success men will find me threatening.	Successful women are interesting and attractive.
If I'm a success I won't need anyone.	Success will bring harmony to my life. I deserve success and beautiful relationships.
People will expect more and more from me and eat me up with expectations.	***I can take care of myself.***
Successful women are unattractive.	Successful women are interesting people. Success adds to my attractiveness.
Successful women don't have good sex lives.	Successful women enjoy whole and wonderful sex lives.

Successful women are bad.

Successful women nuture the planet.

My jewelry isn't good enough to charge a living wage for.

My jewelry is beautiful, sensitive, and personal and of great value.

No one takes me seriously.

People love and appreciate what I have to say.

If I have a successful business it will be my whole life and I won't have any fun.

Success makes for a whole and balanced life.

Men don't like women who do well in business.

Men love successful women.

If I truly put my heart into making my business a success I will be totally destroyed if I fail.

I can lovingly take care of myself. Committment to my work supports all areas of my life.

Successful women dress alike and are boring.

Successful women have the freedom of choice.

Successful women are domineering bitches.

I can **gently** and **lovingly** get what I need.

A woman's place is in the home serving a man.

Listen to your heart. As I follow my heart, I create a beautiful and balanced life.

My only purpose is to meet other people's needs.

I can lovingly say no and take care of myself. As I say no, my yeses become richer.

There is never enough time to do what I need to do.

There is plenty of time to do what I need to do.

I can never tell the whole truth because I need people too much.	I can lovingly say what I need to say.
I will never have a wonderful loving and richly sexual relationship.	**Open your heart and trust.** I deserve a wonderful loving sexual relationship.
I'm too screwed up to love myself well or anyone else.	I'm a loving and generous person.
I'll never grow up.	Trust your process. I grow constantly in beautiful and mature ways.
I give more than I want to customers and friends and don't charge for my time.	Trust your process. Friends and customers respect and value my time highly.

The words crossed out are my editing of this woman's affirmations. Whenever there is a second affirmation for one of her negative statements, it is my addition.

❤ IDEAL PARENT TO SCARED LITTLE KID

When we are little, we often do not get what we want from our parents. then we create hurts, resentments, and negative "tapes" or expectations around this. The sad irony about these negative expectations is that, as we go through life, we are most attracted to people *who would have the most difficulty giving us the very things that we did not get from our parents*. Not only that, we focus much more energy and attention on what these people **do not** give us, than we do on what they do give us. Yet we keep looking for validation outside ourselves, from people who have trouble giving it.

The two-part cure for this (even though I do not believe in "cures") is unfair, but very effective. One, you learn to love your parents more maturely than they loved you when you were little. (i.e., I forgive my parents for their ignorant behavior towards me and I know that underneath their fearful behavior, they love me and want the very best for me.) You learn to love them exactly the way they are and you stop judging them and/or waiting for them to change. (Remember, this does not mean you have to hang around your parents if they are abusive, alcoholic, or negative. Just open your heart to them spiritually.)

Part Two, imagine there is a scared little kid inside you that needs a lot of love appreciation, acknowledgment and reassurance. Ask yourself, "about how old is this little kid?" Then jot down a few notes about what it is like to be that little kid. For example:

> My name is Leonard and I am 5 years old. My mommy and daddy are divorced and I am scared. I do not remember much about my daddy except he is stern, kind of scary, and he used to make me eat peas and egg yolks. I do not see much of my mommy or daddy either one. Now I am six and my mom has boarded out my sister and me to another family. The man works two jobs and the woman is very stern. She threatens me with a ruler for staining my shorts. My first grade teacher jerks me out of my seat by my hair and I do not even know what I did wrong. This is the saddest, loneliest time of my life. I want my mommy and dad to hold me on their laps, hug me, and tell me how much they love me. I want them to tell me how happy they are to have me for their little boy and how proud they are of me. And how they will never leave me and how they will always try to be kind to me even when I make a

mistake or misbehave. I especially need this love, kindness, and reassurance from my daddy.

Next, imagine that you are the perfect parent for this scared little kid. You know exactly what he or she needs. You love and appreciate him tremendously. You will always be there for him and listen to him. You may not always give him exactly what he wants, but you will always take his wishes into consideration.

Now as this ideal parent, write your scared little kid a letter and tell him everything he needs to hear. Give him all he needs as his ideal parent.

Dear Scared Little Leonard,

First of all I want to tell you that I am very proud to have you for a son. You are a source of much joy, delight, and pleasure. Life is a source of joy, delight, and pleasure. And all you have to do is trust me and trust life, and you and I will have great fun and great adventures together. You do not need anything from anyone else. All you need other people for is to give them your love. You have a huge heart, Leonard. It is like a blast furnace. I am very proud of your heart. People can feel the heat of it from 200 feet. You have tons of love to give and all you have to do is give it without expectations and your life will be easy, beautiful, and full of love. And any time you do not get what you want, come to me. I will not **always** give you what you want, but **almost** always. And I will always listen to you. Remember, it is just fine to want things from people. It is only when you expect things from people (positive or negative) that you create pain and suffering. Just ask for what you want from people with no expectations or hidden demands, and, if you do not get what you want, love them and forgive them and come to me. You and I will have such a wonderful time (when you do not get what you want from others) that you will almost be glad you did not get what you wanted originally.

Now, for more specifics about what I love about you. You are very coordinated and quick. I love how fast you sometimes get off your jump shot.

You have developed into a very loving, ethical person. This is one of the things I am most proud of about you.

I love how creative you are with your humor, your intelligence, and your contributions to society and healing the planet. I love how you bring out the best in people and see strengths and beauty in them that even they cannot quite see. I love how you can connect with feelings buried under people's fear and role play them so they can connect with themselves. I love how willing you are to be wrong. I especially love how committed you are to love and forgiveness, to people, family, and work. I love how much of yourself and your money that you donate to people on all levels. I love and am really proud of what a pioneer you are in your field and how you are always searching for more effective ways to help people heal themselves.

I am very proud of how much you lift weights, jog, racewalk, and play basketball. I love how those teens and young adults pick you to be on their teams for "pick up" basketball games. I am proud of how your jump shot has improved since you have been lifting weights.

I love how you can follow the most complicated meanderings of your clients' minds and still follow the thread of their thinking. I love how you can identify with every client that talks to you, how you can love every person that sits across from you.

I love how you keep working on your own growth and never pretend to be a "finished product." I love how open you are with your clients.

I love how much you love your wife and children and how you admit that you are shy and really love them more than you are willing or able to show.

I love how you connect with spiritual wisdom and can make it very practical and relevant in people's lives.

I love how relaxed you are about your income going up and down. And how you put more into doing what you love to do and let the universe support you for it.

I am especially proud of the pioneering work you are doing at the prison and how the men and their families are responding to you there.

Son, do not give up your childlike loving innocence, your willingness to be fooled. I love this quality in you, and your curiosity about life. I love how willing you are to be a student and/or look foolish. I am really proud of this and the courage you have to live this way.

It is hard to imagine having a more wonderful son. You are loving, ethical, committed, and a pure joy to me. I love you with all my heart, and you can always count on that.

Your loving father,

Leonard

Here is another example of quite an impactful letter to a scared little kid. This woman is a therapist and read this to her women's group which led to significant movement for the whole group.

Dearest Little Girl Maria:

I want you to know I love you. I know I've kept you in hiding a lot. I want you to know I am here now. I will always be here for you. I am here to be gentle and kind to you. It is okay for you to be sad. I love being with you. It is absolutely safe for you to come out.

I know how much you were hurt and used when you were little. No one will hurt you or control you like that again. You are a good girl. A nice girl. A gentle girl. I'm so glad to have you.

Please don't be afraid. You don't need to go away again. If you feel you do—if you need to—I'll be here. I'll understand. I'm so proud of you.

I know you were really hurt because your daddy didn't pay attention to you. I know how lonely and sad and empty you felt. I understand. Of course you wanted more of him. I know you were afraid of your mommy. She won't hurt you anymore.

You are safe now. It wasn't your fault, honey. Honestly, you're not bad. They were afraid to see your pain and reach in to you. You did nothing wrong. Really, honey, really. Release your shame. You are so lovable.

I know Peter was hard on you and that you wanted protection from him. I will protect you now. Your grandpa knew you best. I'm glad you had his love. I will take over for him. You will always be safe in my love. You can always trust me. You did your best. I know you love your family and that you needed to hide and to put up a wall. It's over. It's all gone now. I'll be here. No more walls. Nothing to fear.

Take your time, honey. There is no hurry. We are together now. You are not alone any more. No more terrified nights without warm arms to hold you and soothe your fears and nightmares. No more looking and wondering why your love can't be received and why it won't help to stop all the misery, shame, and fear. Your love matters. It's real and you have lots. I'm here to give you the room, the safety, the respect.

You are safe, my child, absolutely safe. Always and forever— always and forever. Let it all go. Release your pain. It's over. Come, darling, take my hand. Walk with me. Surround all of the darkness with light. Illuminate all of the shadows with love.

And, yes, child, if you need more time, more tears, more understanding, it's alright. It's alright. I understand. No one meant to hurt you, abandon you, or abuse you. The world welcomes you now.

Again and again I want to assure you it's all over. You are free. Speak out. Look into my heart and soul. I love you, sweet one, precious one.

Always and forever, always and forever,

Maria

Writing to the scared little child inside you is a powerful process and is a different experience for everyone. You need to be willing to "take what you get" with these processes and keep an open mind. One client (Tom) had quite a struggle with this exercise, though initially he was quite excited when I suggested it. He enclosed the following letter to me when he sent me his letter to his scared little kid. (He also experienced quite a breakthrough shortly after writing these two letters.)

Leonard,

This has turned out to be so much more difficult than I thought it would—I feel a big, horrible knot and numbness right in the middle of my chest and my throat feels tight—I've been feeling this way after I wrote the first sentence. I lost the warm, nourishing enthusiasm and I realize once again just how I have a hard time learning how to really nurture that scared little boy inside of me. As I continued on with the letter, I found myself just blanking out. God only knows where I went. I wanted to deny all that pain, deny all the nurturing I didn't receive, or the unnurturing I did receive.

 Leonard, I don't know if you can use this letter or not—I thought of reworking it, but decided not to. I don't want to reread it right now and be reminded of my loss and my present inability to really get in touch and stay in touch not only with my inner child, but also with those nurturing abilities.

Tom

Dear Tommy,

As my child, I want you to know that you are a precious and wonderful little boy. I want to nurture you, nourish you in every way possible so you can grow to be a confident person with high self-esteem, a boy who, as he grows, learns to care for himself and to have love for others; a boy who feels that I will always be there for you, to support you in all your endeavors; that in your mistakes we can learn together that they really aren't bad or terrible, but rather ways of learning. I want you to always be energetic and full of life—you always have my approval and acceptance. Do what you want and be content, satisfied, happy doing it.

Explore and discover the world and I'll always cherish and love what you find. Love yourself as fully as possible, every moment—in your difficult times, you can turn to me. I'll listen to you. I'll be there for you. If you feel you've done something wrong, I encourage you to talk about it—if not with me, then with a friend.

Have friends, live a full life. Be wild, trust that part of yourself that is savagely gleeful. Do what you really want to do. Love yourself.

Don't be afraid. You can always turn to me when you need to. I'll never abandon you. I'll always love you no matter what you do.

I love you,

Tom

❤ LOVE LETTER TO YOURSELF

The last self-healing exercise is writing a love letter to yourself. Make a list of all your positive traits, qualities, physical attributes, habits, etc. This is not an ego trip. In a very humble way, this is to honor your magnificence. Sometimes it helps to look at yourself objectively as though you are someone else looking at you. You may want to ask friends or loved ones to help you with your list. Then turn this list into a love letter addressed to you and signed by you.

Following is a "love letter to self," by Maria. She reported feeling much resistance to writing this. She had written a long list of things she loved and appreciated about herself but it was several weeks between making the list and writing the letter. She thought it was a little overwhelming to feel really good about herself! Another way people avoid actually completing these processes is they do not sign their letters. Please sign your letters.

Dear Maria,

I have a lot of good feelings about how you are and who you are. I want to share them with you. You are very kind and loving. I know that you really care about people and that you are committed and honest in your relationships. I respect you for how hard you work and for your willingness to be wrong and to learn. You are a growing person and it's exciting and rewarding to share your unfolding.

I love what a good friend you are and how much fun it is to be with you. You are very generous and thoughtful. You are so willing to share everything you have. Your good taste shows in your home, the way you dress, the gifts you give and I love that about you.

You are a good therapist. You always try to give people your best. You tell great stories and use them effectively to help heal the people you see. I love how smart you are and how you pick things up so quickly. I love that you use your humor and personality to make it easy and comfortable for people to face themselves. You deserve your success and I am very proud of you.

I love that you contribute to the healing of the planet. You do it in a lot of ways. You are a good mother and you and your children's relationships inspire people. You are a good wife and that touches people and brings them closer to their power to love. You've worked very hard to be a good daughter and to heal and forgive. Your parents have healed along with you especially as you learned to accept them as they are.

You are a good sister and can be proud of your relationship with your brother.

I love how you love all the people in your life.

You are pretty and I'm glad that you are learning to feel good about yourself and accept your inner beauty. You are vulnerable and it shows and yet you can be tough and I love that balance in you. You are feminine and so soft and passionate. I love your aliveness.

You are magical and your spirituality is blossoming.

I love the way you will celebrate the special meaningful joyous moments in life. I love the way you can dance. It's thrilling when you surrender and let your love and life move through you.   I love you,

Maria

❤ OTHER LETTERS OF HEALING

Anytime you do not get (or are not getting) what you want from someone. There is a powerful healing process available to you. To be effective, however, it must be done with total love. (No malice, no subtle judgments, blame or manipulations.)

Pretend you are the person who is not giving you what you want. Now, as that person, write yourself the perfect letter.

Following is a letter a 30-year-old man wrote to himself at my encouragement. The assignment was "pretend to be your brother, and write you a letter saying all the things you would love to hear from him. Do not write it with malice, or try to make your brother look stupid. Write it with love for both of you."

Dear Roger,

It is very difficult for me to write this letter because I have never been very honest with you and I do not want to face the truth about our relationship. I hope you can forgive me for the way I have treated you. I have always bullied you and never acknowledged you. I got stuck in that position and could not seem to get out of it, even though I felt bad about it.

I resented the special treatment you got as the youngest. I wanted special treatment but I could never be vulnerable enough to ask for it.

I resented how much you loved me and looked up to me. It

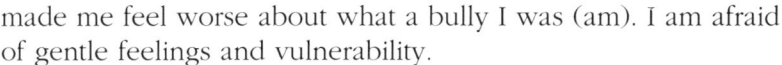

made me feel worse about what a bully I was (am). I am afraid of gentle feelings and vulnerability.

Now comes the hardest part.

I love you, Roger. I always have, I always will and I have always avoided those feelings. I am proud of you. I am proud of what you do, how you live your life and how open you are about your feelings. Your openness scares me and makes me feel inadequate, but I am proud of it. I wish I could be more like you. (That is a feeling I have compulsively avoided my whole life.)

I wish we could sit down sometime and you could tell me all the awful things I did to you so I could admit them and ask for your forgiveness. I would love to lay all of that to rest. I am afraid, though, Roger, that I am still a very frightened, lonely bully who does not have the courage to face all of that.

So, please forgive me and do not expect me to change. Next time we meet I will be the same old bully. Just remember though, underneath all my fearful behavior, I love you, I am proud of you and I am very glad you are my brother.

> Love (much more love than I am willing or able to show),
>
> John

Sometimes the loving thing to do is go ahead and mail a copy of the letter to John (with no expectation of a response). Roger has to use his intuition (the female intuitive side of our personality that bubbles up from deep inside—not the fearful ego that debates like two lawyers in the back of our head). Regarding Roger and John, I sense that it would be loving to send the letter. It is very important to keep a copy for yourself for two reasons.

1. You can re-read the letter if you start to get upset or sad about that relationship and that will re-ground you in the universe of love; and

2. If the person to whom you sent the letter gets upset, it is nice to have a copy of exactly what you did write.

Here is another example of writing a letter to yourself that you would love to get from someone else. This is especially healing for couples. This couple's intimacy had been fading a bit. They had been together over two years and their old tapes had subtly started weakening their relationship. When the routines of the day were handled and they headed for bed, the wife was retreating more and more into reading. The husband's old tapes about love, intimacy and women, were playing louder and louder in his head. When he consulted me, I suggested the letter writing process and this is what he came up with.

> My Dear Love,
>
> You are a wonderful man and the perfect man for me. One part of me wants you close and one part of me wants to keep you away.
>
> I love it when we are close and kiss a lot. I love it when you kiss me all over, play with my breasts and genitals and make love to me. I love it when you are inside me, thrusting, and we are both getting more and more excited. These are some of the most wonderful moments of my life. I dearly desire to give up my control and surrender to all that beauty and magnificence that we create together.
>
> Sadly there is another part of me (a stronger part right now) that is terrified of all that. (I am also afraid we are losing all that.) Anyway, this stronger part of me is more comfortable avoiding our love and passion. I feel safer keeping you distant, unpassionaate, not touching my breasts and genitals. I love to read but I also feel safer reading than making love. In a weird kind of guilty way I also feel safer when I have herpes.
>
> Anyway, I just want you to keep on loving me and forgiving me. I want to work on this and I am very scared. I don't know which scares me the most—overcoming it or not overcoming it. I love you with all my heart. I wish I could make a strong

promise about this but I can't. Thank you for your love and patience. You are a miracle in my life and I don't want to let you just sit there.

Your Snicklefritz

She read it out loud to him. They both cried and moved closer to healing and intimacy. The husband kept practicing loving his wife exactly the way she was, asking for what he wanted with no demands or manipulations and their sexual and emotional contact increased. A few months later she wrote him the following note on a sweet romantic card.

My Precious Bear,

This seems like the perfect card to describe how life seems with you. I'm so glad that you are my husband. You are more than I could ever dream of. I couldn't ask for more. I want us to continue "fine-tuning" our marriage. I want to learn to treat you with the love, respect, and appreciation you always deserve all the time. I want our sex life to be as exciting and sweet as we both desire.

For keeps,

Your Sweetheart

These letters you write to yourself are crucial for your healing. You must provide this for yourself. Otherwise you will spend the rest of your life waiting for your mate, boss, and/or parents to give you what you did not get when you were a small child. (And not "letting it in" when they do give it.)

❤ FURTHER WORK IN LOVE AND FORGIVENESS

For those of you seeking further support for this work, I recommend the following:

Mini Course For Healing Relationships And Bringing About Peace of Mind by G.G. Jampolsky, M.D. (Send $9 to Mini Course, P.O. Box 1012, Tiburon, CA 94920). Sold in bookstores for $8.

Here are the six principles underlying the Mini Course

1. One of the main purposes of time is to enable us to choose what we want to experience. ***Do we want to experience peace or do we want to experience conflict?***

2. All minds are joined and are one.

3. What we perceive through our physical senses presents us with a limited and distorted view of reality.

4. We really cannot change the world we live in or other people. We can change how we perceive the world, how we perceive others and how we perceive ourselves.

5. There are only two emotions: one is love and the other is fear. Love is our true reality; fear is something our mind has made up and is therefore unreal.

6. What we experience is our state of mind projected outward. If our state of mind is one of well-being, love and peace, then that is what we will project and therefore experience. If our state of mind is one filled with doubt, fear and concern about illness, then we will project this state outward, and it will therefore be our experiential reality.

If you start the 18-day Mini Course, I recommend that you ***finish it no matter what!*** You may run into a friend that "needs it more than you do," but that is just your ego trying to avoid this gentle, powerful wisdom. As you are doing the Course, if you come to a card that has special meaning to you and you want to stay with that card for 2 or 3 days, that is fine. It has become a 20-day course at that point, instead of 18 days.

An excellent book to further this work is *Prescriptions For Happiness* by Ken Keyes, Jr.   Ken has three prescriptions for happiness and the entire book is a discussion of these three.

1. Ask for what you want but do not demand it.

2. Accept whatever happens, for now.

3. When you do not get what you want, turn up (increase) your love.

 Most of us can turn up our love when we are getting what we want. Really powerful people, who can transform difficult situations, are the ones who can turn up their love and commitment when they are not getting what they want. Remember too, that in some circumstances, the most loving thing to do is to refuse (lovingly refuse) to interact or participate with someone who is engaged in addictive behavior (i.e., alcohol or drug abuse, negative gossip, illegal behavior, overeating). As you walk away, remember to repeat over and over in your head "I love you, I forgive you, I bless you, I release you."

Another excellent book for furthering this work is called *You Can Have It All*, by Arnold Patent, published by Money Mastery, Box 336, Piermont, NY 10968.

More recommended readings are listed in of my newsletters in the appendix (pages 85 and 100) .

❤ *Love and Forgiveness*

❤ APPENDIX

Compilation of Themes Written in Past Eight Years

❤ ABSTRACT

I have been in private practice for 14 years, introduced Gestalt Therapy to the Northwest in 1967, and practiced it for 11 years. My work changed significantly in September of 1978, and the following comments reflect these changes.

Most people experience life as though they are their ego and they are their body. (And their mind and their feelings.)

There is another view/experience where your ego and body are companions on your journey, but you are not your ego and you are not your body. There is tremendous peace that comes with this awareness and, paradoxically, a freedom to be even more richly involved with life, people, and experiences.

Most therapies maintain that old traumas need to be felt, expressed, experienced or understood, deliver undelivered communications, release pent-up feelings, etc. Much of this is unnecessary (from this other view/experience of which I speak).

The key, really, to letting go of the past (or dropping the past as a "prison") is *forgiveness*. Forgiveness is the healing of the "perception" of separation.

(This is my fourth version of this paper in the past six months, and I have avoided discussing forgiveness even though it is crucial because people have so many naive "pictures" in their heads about it.)

Forgiveness is a source of power. Forgiveness gives more to the forgiver than to the forgivee. Forgiveness turns liabilities into assets. Like Einstein's scientific genius, forgiveness turns your very "stuck point" or greatest obstacles into solutions, support and a source of power. You can tell if you have truly forgiven someone because you will feel a connection and a peace with them that you have never felt before.

The content that people bring to therapy has not changed that much (i.e., health, fears, life situations and relationships). My focus is different, however. The biggest similarity with the way I used to work is that I still emphasize "the truth shall set you free." Beyond that, I have reduced my tendency to Gestalt old traumas, work with dreams, fantasies, guided imagery (with a few self-healing exceptions) or get really into the details of the past or current situations. I teach people how to see "problems" in terms of attachments, illusions and their ego creating a false sense of control.

The difficulty with writing and discussing this is that these activities (writing and discussing) are almost always left hemisphere. The quality of experience (that these words point towards) is a synchronized right and left hemisphere experience. The other difficulty is that most of us have known for years that all human suffering can be traced to attachments, but that is knowledge. To paradoxically surrender to this truth and experience the many ego deaths that accompany this surrender, leads to wisdom. There is a vast difference between wisdom and knowledge. I hope to help people get a glimpse of this difference in my work and see the dramatic changes this can lead to.

❤ "CHRISTMAS BLUES"

You Can't Change Events and People But You Can Change How You Feel About Them

From *Seattle Post Intelligencer,* December 2, 1980

This time of year tends to stir up unfinished business with the ego. (That part of you that attaches too much significance to your importance as an individual and dramatizes your feelings.) The Christmas holidays seem to trigger people's feelings of abandonment, loss and grief. Also, this is a time of warmth and cheer, and this reminds people of the warmth and cheer that is missing in their lives, and/or has been missing in the past. More importantly, however, our egos are often attracted to focusing on what is (or has been) missing in our lives, and Christmas therefore provides an opportunity for this negative focus.

There is another way of dealing with all of this that can be very healing and exciting. Instead of looking at what we don't have or didn't have in the past (as our ego often prefers*), we can look at (and learn to experience) what we do have on a spiritual level. (Relax, now, I am not on a religion trip. I am just talking about a spiritual level of existence where everything is more fun and nothing is such a big deal. Most of us have had glimpses of this space and the feelings of prosperity and well-being that accompany it, and I am telling you that it is possible to spend extended periods of time there and eventually experience it as your "normal" state.)

So, instead of focusing on the pain of the past, you can choose to feel the prosperity of the present. One of the main tools in this process is forgiveness.

*There is a bit more to this that is worth explaining. Actually, our egos carry around negative expectations from the past and search for evidence in the present to fit our old scripts (or expectations). The universe is flexible and will provide evidence to fit any script if you look hard enough. And as most of us know and are reluctant to admit, our egos are very creative and ingenious at interpreting the "facts" to support a particular feeling that we are attached to.

❤ Who Haven't You Forgiven?

Negative behavior comes from fear and insecurity and is actually a state of ignorance. Whatever people did or did not do to you (or with you) in the past (yesterday or 12 or 20 years ago) that was a source of pain for you, did not have that much to do with you, but was more an expression of their own fear and insecurity (or sometimes an innocent preference). As long as you continue to take it personally or as a sign of your own un-lovable-ness, you will feel "done to." When you forgive them for their ignorant or innocent behavior towards you, you will feel a peaceful connection with them, an appreciation of them and an inner peace that you did not know was possible.

Now, I am not talking about "stuffing" or suppressing your anger about the incident or situation. You can have your anger if you wish. What I am saying is that for some people it is very rich and freeing to look at anger as an **unnecessary state of ignorance**. If you want to be free of it, ask yourself, "What am I afraid of?" and "Who haven't I forgiven?"

Forgiveness heals the illusion of separateness. You are a part of the energy of all things. When you are aware of this, you feel a paradoxical peacefulness that allows you to be more richly involved with people and events while at the same time realizing that those people and events do not determine your peace and happiness. They are only the frosting on the cake. (And when you are not overinvested in them, they taste better than ever!)

The more that you can forgive and let go of your past, the more of you that is available to **be here now**. That is the single most important factor in being able to experience prosperity, healing and peace of mind.

❤ LETTING GO

"You are attached to the past."

"Yes, I know that."

"You are attached to your problems."

"I know. I understand that!"

"Right now you are in your head. How would you like to get so close to letting go of the past and letting go of your problems that you would be right on the brink? You would get glimpses of what it would be like to let go. You would experience how attached you really are to the past and to your problems. You would see how you choose moment after moment after moment, all day long, to hang on to the past rather than be fresh and alive and brand new, right here now."

"I don't know if I would like that or not."

"Well, once you get that close, you will never be able to take your problems quite as seriously again. And if you surrender, and go over the brink, you will discover a beauty in your everyday life that will amaze you. It is a very humbling and freeing experience.

We create this experience for people in our seminars and groups. We also teach about "effort" as a barometer and about the absolutely empowering nature of commitment. Forgiveness and commitment have something in common as seen by our ego. The ego thinks that to forgive or commit means you are giving something up or giving something away. Actually you are reclaiming a tremendous amount of personal power. We are committed to making our seminars powerful, light hearted, humorous and healing for you. And we teach what we need to learn.

❤ HOW TO LEAVE ROOM FOR MORE MONEY TO SHOW UP IN YOUR LIFE

Drop the thought that you have to earn a living. Life is a gift and everything you need exists already at this present moment. You do not need to earn a living; you do, however, need to open yourself up to *serving* and *being served*. Idleness is folly but it is just as foolish to look upon work as drudgery, slavery or something that you have to do. It is an opportunity to serve and to express your love no matter how indirect that may seem to you at times. To hold work in any other light is to invite contagious negativity into your life and undermine your joy, prosperity and peace of mind.

•Drop scarcity consciousness. (There is not enough love, money, water, mashed potatoes, ice cream, etc.)

•Drop competitive thinking and action. Avoid bragging, it tends to cancel joy and accomplishments. Money is not power. The mind is power.

•Drop the fear of expenditure. Spending money is exchanging ideas and energy. Be grateful for the convenience of it. There is no loss of substance, only a continual exchange.

•Act as though your good is at hand and it will be so.

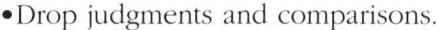

•Drop judgments and comparisons.

Associate yourself with persons who are prosperous. Not necessarily rich, but generous people who have surrendered to the flow of the universe and the above-mentioned wisdom. Go often into environments of beauty and luxury. Learn to purchase things at better stores even if they are only small items at first.

Right now you might be thinking "you tell me not to judge and compare and then you tell me to hang out with prosperous people and shop in better stores. It sounds snobby to me!" You can lovingly discriminate for your own growth and evolution without being snobby and judgmental about it. There is an important difference here.

Rejoice always in success, wherever you find it. To envy another quickly undermines our own prosperity. It helps to remember that we are part of the energy of all things, so we are a part of any success we see.

If you see something beautiful in a store, don't say "I can't afford it." Just stop and enjoy it. Claim it as part of you. Then release it.

All of this wisdom on abundance applies to relationships and achievements as well as money.

Remember, if you seldom get involved with others, if you seldom accept new ideas and people, if you only go to familiar places, you are probably manifesting consciousness of lack. There is no virtue in not having what you need for a joyous healthy life.

❤ CHANGE YOUR THINKING

Regular study of affirmative thoughts will produce affirmative circumstances in your life, because whatever you think about regularly will tend to become a part of your experience. Therefore, if you begin to uplift your thinking, to focus on what's good and right about yourself, others and the world, you will start attracting better things into your life. Whether you desire improved health, more prosperity, happier relationships, or a deeper understanding of your own nature, you can have it by changing the way you think.

Your mind is like a magic greenhouse, whatever you allow in it or put in it, is going to grow and start to manifest itself in your life whether it is scarcity, illness and gloom or prosperity, health and joy.

Affirmations

You can say I can or you can say I can't, you'll be accurate either way.

Today I accept more success, health and happiness into my life than I accepted yesterday. And I welcome change, for it offers me new opportunities to express the Life-Force which moves through me. I am thankful for change.

1. Use present tense (acknowledging that everything is created first on the mental plane before it manifests in objective reality). Don't say "I will have a new car," say "I now have a new car."

2. Short and simple is better.

3. Choose affirmations that feel right for you.

4. (This one is extremely important) "Affirmations are not meant to contradict or try to change your feelings or emotions. It is important to accept and experience all your feelings, including so-called 'negative' ones, without attempting to change them. At the same time, affirmations can help you create a new point of view about life which will enable you to have more and more satisfying experiences from now on."*

5. When stating affirmations, suspend all doubts and create the feeling that *they can be true*. Allow yourself to feel for the moment that you have the power to create that reality. (Which you do!) "You can say 'I can' or you can say 'I can't.' You'll be accurate either way." Henry Ford.

6. Visualizing your affirmations increases their power.

7. Including references to spiritual sources increases the power of affirmations (Universal love, divine intelligence, the light within me, Buddha, Christ, God) if you are comfortable with it.

*From *Creative Visualization* by Shakti Gawain

Here are some useful sample affirmations.

- It's okay for me to have everything I want!
- This is a rich universe and there's plenty for all of us.
- Abundance is my natural state of being. I accept it now!
- Infinite riches are now freely flowing into my life.
- Everyday I am growing more financially prosperous.
- The more I have, the more I have to give.
- The more I give, the more I receive, and the happier I feel.
- It's okay for me to have fun and enjoy myself, and I do!
- I am now enjoying everything I do!
- I feel happy and blissful just being alive.
- I am open to receiving all the blessings of this abundant universe!
- All things are now working together for good in my life.
- I give thanks now for my life of health, wealth, happiness, and perfect self-expression.

Much of what I have learned about prosperity comes from Jerry Jampolsky, *Teach Only Love*, Shakti Gawain, *Creative Visualization*, and Carrick-Cook "Keys to Prosperity," Oct. 83, *Science of Mind*.

❤ TORONTO INTERVIEW

Revised Leonard Shaw Interview for Ron Osea in Toronto
Edited and Interpreted by Robin Brown, January 1983

1. How would you describe what you do as a therapist, as a teacher, a guide?

As a teacher/facilitator and fellow human being, I help people feel better about their lives, relationships and work. I help them feel really good about just being alive.

2. How does this role fit into the context of your seminar, your relationship with participants?

I do this in weekend seminars where 50 to 100 people gather for four 3-to 4-hour sessions from Friday night through Sunday afternoon. In these seminars I teach by helping participants to take a much more light-hearted approach to their lives. People tell me areas of their lives where they have difficulty and then I help them see how they are getting in their own way. I do this in an atmosphere of ease and acceptance.

3. How can people actually reveal their innermost thoughts in front of a room full of strangers? What if I am too intimidated to participate?

Within the climate of acceptance, the honesty, intensity, caring and support increases moment by moment. Sharing of one's thoughts/feelings comes naturally and always depends on the individual's choice. It's a very powerful experience to reveal oneself with the support of a large group. And, being witness to another's honesty is equally profound. However, it is not necessary to show yourself in order to get great benefit from the seminar.

4. What about people who have no major issues to deal with?

By 'letting go' of the serious, problematic focus of one's thoughts, ideas, feelings, one is free to experience health, beauty, joy and well-being in everyday life. The seminar experience increases your respect and appreciation for everything—loved ones, co-workers and ourselves. It's like you learn about and practice implementing your own power and well-being, both mental and physical. So you do not need a heavy problem to benefit from the seminar. People who come for the experience gain a tremendous amount of energy and rejuvenated happiness as they recognize and appreciate existing feelings of well-being.

5. How does your approach differ from other therapies, analyses, etc.?

Basically, for the past four years, I have assumed that there are only two emotions—love and fear. And I don't deal with the past, the negative, fearful feelings as much as I did the first 15 years that I practiced psychotherapy.

6. How did you develop this approach? What is your background in this field?

As an ACSW with a master's degree from the University of Washington, I have 19 years' experience practicing individual, group and family therapy from a variety of perspectives, i.e., Freudian—Existential—Gestalt. The last four years I have been doing this 'letting go,' 'nothing's a big deal.' 'everything's more fun' kind of therapy in my private practice and seminars in Canada, Germany, Denmark and Seattle. I have come to realize that people do not need to therapize their negativity, talk about it, relive it, etc. What I am saying is that 80 to 90 percent of our negative feelings do not need to be discussed/explained. We can just drop them. We can retrain our minds. Otherwise, we run the risk of making negativity a larger part of our daily existence. The mind is like a magic greenhouse. Whatever is put in it, or allowed in it, is going to multiply. So, a lot of what I do is re-orienting seminar participants to 'let go' of that 80 to 90 percent of energy caught up in negativity and replace that with well-being, honesty, forgiveness, commitment and loving. The other 10 percent we still talk about, but that may only be because I am not high enough to see beyond it.

7. What do you want people to know about your work?

My seminars involve a medley of honest, liberating experiences which are exciting, full of love, and touch one's simple, yet often ignored, human nature.

8. What do you feel is the most important aspect of your work?

Well, that is to help people realize the main reason they are on this planet is to give and receive love. And nothing else matters as much as we think it does. The main tools for helping people to realize this are forgiveness, commitment, surrender or letting go, and realizing there are only two emotions, love and fear. My work is simpler now and more powerful than ever.

9. What would you like to tell people about forgiveness, commitment and letting go?

Forgiveness and commitment, although they initially feel like giving in, giving up or losing, truly result in more energy and acceptance of life: that in forgiving and committing, we are really 'letting go' of negativity and facing the truth about ourselves and actually reclaiming our personal power. Forgiveness, commitment and surrender are EMPOWERING!

10. What one thing above all else should people know?

Most people feel like their life is running them, and the seminars help people realize that they are making their life exactly the way it is, and they can make it different.

❤ EFFORT AND COMMITMENT (1983)

(Two things that I have learned a lot about lately)

"If it's an effort, you're missing it." —Meaning if life at any particular moment is an effort, you've lost your connection with inner peace. (That paradoxical space where nothing matters as much as we think it does—and everything tastes better)

or

you are in your little mind instead of your big mind

or

you've lost touch with the feeling that you are part of the energy of all things

or

you've lost touch with (squeezed yourself off from) the infinite flow of love that is always present in the universe

or

you can see the drop of water in the ocean but you can't see the ocean in the drop of water.

So, if life is an effort at any particular moment, you might as well slow down, back off, breathe deeply and let go of your ego attachments. In doing this you will find a powerful reservoir of solutions that you could not see moments before and things will unfold much more smoothly and effortlessly. (Even if things look messy on the surface you will see their underlying perfection.)

In my work I maximize (to the best of my abilities) the opportunity for people to eventually find that space inside themselves and realize (to quote Jampolsky's *Mini Course*) "My peace comes only from within me, it cannot come from anywhere else." When I say realize, I do not mean intellectually realize, I mean experientially surrender—a postive giving in to love.

(The first time I wrote this material was in an early morning letter to my friend Dudley Strasburg who was arranging for me to do a seminar in Wiesbaden Germany. By this point in the letter I was beginning to feel a natural high. Colors were vivid in my room and I was forgetting how to spell.)

The other thing I want to share is that I have something very powerful to teach about commitment but I'm not sure what I want to say about it because I am still learning from it. And as I am writing (riding) (there goes my natural high again) this right now, I'm seeing "commitment to myself" and "commitment to the now." I experience some dilemmas here. You see, when I totally commit myself to my mate, she immediately becomes more beautiful to me inside and out and I can see her perfection. So right now as I am on the verge of total commitment to myself, I am experiencing a few awarenesses that I feel reluctant to share, such as—I have been more committed to my mate than I have to myself. Also—if I am not committed fully to myself, how could I be fully committed to my mate because I would not be telling her the full truth about myself. This is getting very exciting and scary.

And I am also feeling on the verge of a whole new commitment to the now. (By this point everything in my room is almost vibrating it is so vivid). I am feeling very close to my friends, clients, family, myself, the exhaust of the VW that just drove by, the micro-organisms living on my eyelashes, etc., etc., etc. Tears are welling up as they often do when we "come home."

P.S. Since writing the above, I have been able to stop in most any set of circumstances and get into and soak up the now, as I never have before. It is powerful, a wonderful feeling of prosperity, a little overwhelming and often leaves me a little misty-eyed. Also, in case you are wondering, forgiveness and surrender are still very important in my world. Forgiveness heals the illusion of separateness and is the tool you use until it is no longer necessary.

❤ RELATIONSHIPS

There is a change showing up in our culture that affects couples, families, friendships, work, politics, the arts and much more. It takes the form of a deeper involvement and commitment by people and it has transformational possibilities for those involved.

What makes it transformational is a willingness to keep breathing, loving, and telling the truth about your experience when you feel helpless, hopeless, ungrounded and getting no agreement from others. It takes a willingness to see the very best in people when they are showing their worst, and to know that "the bigger the disaster, the bigger the opportunity." It also helps to know the difference between transformation and masochism.

Your most pressing irritations, frustrations or fears often offer your most empowering path. This is one of the most exciting aspects of relationships, especially primary relationships. The things that bother you the most about relationships (or life) are the very situations or dynamics that can propel you to a higher level of peace, power and happiness.

This approach takes courage, action and commitment. This does not work as a technique or trick to get what you want or manipulate your partner. Yet, if you truly hold it in your heart, that every obstacle is here to serve you, then you will create that experience in your day-to-day living and loving.

Watch out though, because your ego will want to turn all this into a technique to more subtly maintain control and manipulate the meeting of your needs without risking.

Forgiveness and commitment have something in common as seen by our ego. The ego thinks that to forgive or commit means you are giving something up or giving something away. Actually you are reclaiming a tremendous amount of personal power.

To teach this takes continual surrender, commitment, ego death and freshness on the part of the therapist. It is an inspiring and energizing way of life.

"Until one is committed, there is hesitancy, the chance to draw back, always ineffectiveness. Concerning all acts of initiative(and creation), there is one elementary truth the ignorance of which kills countless ideas and splendid plans: that the moment one definitely commits oneself, then Providence moves too. All sorts of things occur to help one that would never otherwise have occurred. A whole stream of events issues from the decision, raising in one's favor all manner of unforeseen incidents and meetings and material assistance which no one could have dreamed would have come their way. Whatever you can do or dream you can do, begin it. Boldness has genius, power and magic in it. Begin it now."

—*Murray and Goethe*

❤ THE COUPLES CONTRACT

Date_____

We, _____,
do hereby commit ourselves to having an open, honest, vulnerable, loving, _____, _____, _____,

relationship with each other.

We acknowledge our contribution to each others pain and ask for forgiveness. We take a stand that those painful experiences will make a significant contribution to our wisdom, sensitivity, compassion and to our commitment to our loving relationship.

We also commit ourselves to working on our own growth as individuals and to practice loving each other exactly the way we are. We agree to keep reaching within for our higher loving selves, regardless of the provocative, painful, _____, _____, _____ circumstances that show up in our lives or in our behavior with each other.

❤ *Love and Forgiveness*

We agree not to support, contribute to, or participate in any of the following toxic or addictive behaviors with each other:

_____

_____

_____

_____

We agree and commit ourselves to do the following homework _____ times in _____ days, by _____ date.

☐ The "one thing I like about you is _____", (said once); "One thing I think we agree on is _____", (said once); and "One thing I want you to know about me is _____", (said for four minutes). Remember, **no response** or feedback to each other on the content of this exercise.

☐ The Masters and Johnson sexual exercises _____ times in

_____ days, by _____ date.

☐ The "free association" exercise _____ times in _____ days, by _____ date.

☐ The four minutes of silent eye contact with slow, deep breathing and sharing afterwards _____ times in _____ days, by _____ date.

Signed and Dated:_____ _____

Witness:_____

❤ ANOTHER UNIVERSE

There is a very powerful place (another universe) that surrounds you and has existed your whole life. Most of us overlook this universe because we pay so much attention to the everyday universe where we stub our toe, get our feelings hurt, get angry, etc.

If we pay attention to (visualize) the powerful universe, it becomes more and more real and eventually we see and experience it as the most real of all the universes.

This is the universe where we all love each other absolutely and unconditionally. It has always been there, waiting to support and nourish us. The presence of this universe is very threatening to our ego for several reasons.

1. It does not make sense. This universe is beyond "making sense," and our ego is addicted to "making sense."

2. When we visualize ourselves in this universe, we often see that all we need to do is let go of certain negative attitudes and behaviors, and the love, power and abundance (we claim we want) would start showing up in our everyday lives.

3. Our ego would rather be right than happy.

4. We often have to forgive someone (as opposed to "understanding" them) to shift into the universe of unconditional love.

I need to caution you now that your ego will also try to turn this powerful wisdom into a trick or technique to manipulate your desires from the world (or from your mate especially) and that will backfire. You need to notice this urge, let it be, and then step into the universe of unconditional love.

Spending time in this universe will transform your life.

You will find it easier to say no to people.

You will find it easier to speak from your heart.

You will find it easier to say yes to people.

You will find it easier to spot all your negative tendencies yet not indulge them.

As an experiment, next time you are in conflict with someone and they are being negative or manipulative, step into the universe of unconditional love. Instead of constructing your counter argument or point of view, remind yourself that underneath their negativity (fear) your companion loves you absolutely and unconditionally. It will have an amazing impact on you and your relationship. This is a very powerful experience and usually most powerful with your mate and/or parents.

If you had some rough times with your parents, or even if they beat you or abandoned you, this all applies even more powerfully. Underneath all of their destructive or abandoning behavior, they always have and always will love you absolutely and unconditionally. If you ever own that love and let it in, you will never be the same person. (That usually means a lot of letting go, for your ego.)

One last important point. When you visualize yourself in the universe of unconditional love, you must visualize it like it is alive and real and **yours right now**. (It is, by the way.) You are basking in the middle of it **right now**. And you are radiating your unconditional love to others right now. This is quite important. (Do not be surprised if powerful insights show up during this process.)

❤ LOVE AND FORGIVENESS ARE POWER POLITICS

People involved in political issues often think that a significant portion of their strength and power comes from indignation and "putting down" the opposition. Actually people would be 20 or 100 times more powerful coming from a space of love and forgiveness instead of anger and judgment. That is how Gandhi did it.

"Well, he was unusual. I am no Gandhi," you might say. We are much closer to Gandhi's level than we realize. We all have that potential within us, and our life would be more beautiful (powerful) if we made use of it.

Most of us would rather be right than get what we want. We would rather be indignant than make the world a better place.

"Not me," you say. "I can see it in my brother-in-law or boss or mate, but I really try."

All that means is that you have become so slick in your position, that you have fooled yourself. Our brother-in-law boss or mate do not see that they would rather be right than happy (get what they want). Is not it possible therefore that we do not see the same folly in ourselves?

Every indignation or judgment we create helps maintain the conflict or problem that we claim we want to remedy. The power and wisdom of that statement is tremendously difficult for our ego to accept. It is our ego or "little mind" that would actually rather be right than happy. Our "little mind" runs on fear, insecurity and scarcity (there is not enough money, not enough dessert, not enough love or time). In our "big mind" we already know everything written in this article. Unfortunately, the way we are socialized and educated, strengthens our little mind and pushes our big mind into the background and disuse.

Every bit of our righteousness or indignation creates an alienation that poisons us and poisons the planet. Every time we forgive, we heal that alienation, dissolve that poison, and increase our personal power immensely.

People are confused about forgiveness. They associate it with weakness and letting people "get away with it." People think that if you forgive someone they are apt to "get you" again. The paradox here is that actually the opposite is true. Forgiveness decreases the chances of a repeat, and indignation actually increases the chances of the problem repeating itself or continuing. Our very indignation helps repeat or recreate the problem. (And our indignant ego would actually be disappointed if the problem was solved or resolved.) The ego is an indignation machine waiting to react. Some of us are noisy about it like Archie Bunker, and some of us are sneaky and arrogant about it and keep it to ourselves. Most of us fall between those two extremes.

❤ Love and Forgiveness

Forgiveness heals the illusion of separateness. We are all in this together. The president of the chemical company that dumps waste where we do not want it, is our lost brother or sister. If we confront them from a space of love and forgiveness, we will be much more effective and powerful. We will feel so grounded, peaceful and strong that we will wonder "Who am I anyway? Where did all this strength come from?" Honestly, when you get beyond your ego, you feel like the ocean is backing you up! And you feel that you are on the same team as the person you are confronting.

This applies to the person who cuts in front of us in traffic, leaves candy wrappers in our yard, smokes alongside us at work, is a non-smoker, steals our radio or car or mate. This applies to Ted Bundy. If we come from love and forgiveness we realize that to put Bundy in jail is a loving thing to do for him. To drive the British out of India is a loving thing to do for the British. This may sound "airy-fairy" but it is very practical and can transform our everyday life from greyness and effort into joy, enthusiasm and excitement.

One woman with whom I counseled was a labor negotiator for 18,000 people. when she started practicing this wisdom, it took 95% of the tension out of her work and increased her power as a negotiator remarkably.

Most people I counsel experience a drastic reduction of activity in their "indignation machine" (ego) when they forgive their parents. (We think we have achieved this when usually we have only understood and figured out our parents.) Most indignation we create in our daily lives actually stems from being unforgiving (incomplete) with our parents. As Dr. Jerry Jampolsky says in *Love Is Letting Go of Fear*, "I am never upset for the reason I think." It can be quite liberating to repeat daily to ourselves "I forgive my parents and others for their ignorant (innocent) behavior towards me."

So if we want to "take action" involving drunk drivers, rapists, the secret police or a so-called opposing political party, we would be much more powerful (and increase the chances of getting what we want) if we come from a space of love and forgiveness.

This is not a trick to be accomplished in our head. It is a surrender of the heart. We can tell when we have accomplished it because we will feel a peaceful connection with our "opponent." We will feel a bit like they are our lost brother or sister and we have healed the alienation.

If we cannot accomplish this, then the most healing thing we can do is to acknowledge to people close to us that we "refuse to forgive the 'opponent' for their ignorant behavior towards us (and others), ***even though we know our unforgiveness helps maintain the problem we claim we want to remedy***."

Being that honest and that responsible will automatically move things in a healing direction.

❤ POSITION PAPER 1987

"What's the bottom line?"

"Unconditional love."

"Oh, God, here we go with that unconditional pie in the sky love stuff. (It irritates me and/or makes me feel inadequate.) Sometimes life just sucks or some people are just jerks."

"Nope, it's all a reflection of you. And I'm going to teach you all about it so you can be happy, peaceful, grateful and joyful most of the time. This is beyond psychotherapy, beyond problems, this is very practical empowering wisdom that you can use every day in any situation.(The more difficult the situation, the more benefits to the practice.)

"What do you mean by beyond problems?"

"Talking about problems is a way of withholding love from others and of course ultimately from yourself. The universe is so full of love and abundance that we have to work extra hard to ignore it and shut it out.The main way we do this is to create (and dwell on) problems."

"So by complaining about how my boss underpays me and mismanages the business, I am withholding love from myself?"

"Yes."

"Do you mind if I throw up now?"

"Go right ahead."

"Joking aside, I don't get it."

"You don't have to get it and you don't have to believe in it. If you want results in your life, just practice this wisdom."

Let go of your judgments and practice loving your boss (or your mate) exactly the way they are. When you do this you will actually be loving a part of yourself that you have been withholding love from for a long time. It is a very healing experience.

Another way you can practice is —next time your boss or your mate is on their soap box expressing their point of view, instead of rehearsing your view in your head, try repeating over and over in your mind, "I love you —I believe you. I love you —I believe you." Not that you agree with them but just that you believe that what they are saying is real for them.

Experiment with it. There are some fascinating benefits to it. Also, if someone has been using or abusing you, practicing this wisdom increases the likelihood that you will confront them in a loving, non-judgmental manner (which always gets better results than indignation and blame).

There are no exceptions to the applicability of this wisdom, and it is usually hardest to practice with your mate, children and parents (which makes them your most powerful teachers).

I love teaching this, so feel free to call me if you want some coaching. I often have half (25 min.) sessions with people once they catch onto it.

❤ I WISH I HAD WARNED THEM

Newsletter, November, 1987

Occasionally a couple comes for help in a sad state. One of them (usually the husband) is desperate and will do anything to save the relationship. The other one (usually the wife) has given up and just wants out of the relationship with minimum pain to both. Sometimes she is in love with someone else, but often she is just tired of not getting what she wants. She feels like something has died and it is too late to do anything about it. I feel "If only I had talked to them sooner, maybe we could have saved this relationship." The following short story is my attempt to "talk to you sooner."

The Sleeping Husband

Joan says one or more of the following:

"Honey, we don't make love often enough."

"We need to improve our communication."

"Let's go to a counselor."

"You don't need me, you just need your work."

"We never go out any more."

Howard says one or more of the following:

"I have a headache. I'm exhausted."

"You are right, let's do it tonight."

"It costs too much, let's just go out to dinner."

"Of course I need you. Why do you think I am doing all of this?"

"I like staying home with you."

If Joan insists, there is an improvement in talk or sex or socializing that lasts from one day to three weeks. But she does not feel Howard is very excited about it, she feels he does it to appease her, and soon things are back to Howard working long hours and reading the paper or watching TV.

This pattern could last 2 years, or 10 years, until the day Joan says she is moving out or wants a divorce, even though she loves Howard and wants him to be happy. (Sometimes she has lost touch with her feelings of love.)

In extreme cases, Howard has been pretty happy (asleep) up to this point. His wife, kids and secretary go crazy around him, but he feels on top of things.

So, when Joan says, "I am moving out" and Howard cannot talk her out of it, he finally says, "Let's go talk to Leonard." She may say, "No, I am finally going after what I want and I don't need help." Or she may say yes because she knows Howard is going to go through hell and will need all the help he can get. Seldom does she say yes, she wants to revive and heal the relationship.

On the surface it looks like Howard is the one with the problem. Actually they are both hiding their fears by judging their mate. Often they are afraid of intimacy. In this example Howard is fearful of intimacy, feels inadequate and does not even know it. Joan is afraid of it, too, but can hide her fear behind Howard's symptoms and she may not even know she is also afraid.

If the above scenario fits you or just makes you nervous, you may want to take some action. There is no substitute for **COURAGE and ACTION**.

You do not have to go to a therapist to breathe new life into your marriage or turn your relationship around. To save time and money, here is what you can do for $8 or $10:

Buy one of the following books and read aloud to each other and discuss it. Do this twice a week for 40 to 60 minutes for one month. That's it! Pretty simple, isn't it. But you will be surprised at all the things you will put ahead of it. **THIS IS AN EMERGENCY!** You have a disaster brewing in your nest. Unless you have a water pipe break, do not let anything interfere with this special time together!

You Can Have It All • by Arnold Patent

Prescriptions for Happiness • by Ken Keyes, Jr.

A Conscious Person's Guide to Relationships • by Ken Keyes, Jr.

The Joy of Sex • by Alex Comfort, M.D., Ph.D.

Life Is A Game of Choices • by Jennifer James, Ph.D.

Teach Only Love • by Gerald Jampolsky, M.D.

Dr. Ruth's Guide for Married Lovers • by Ruth Westheimer, Ph.D.

Creative Visualization • by Shakti Gawain

Remember, too, problems are opportunities in disguise, and every negative experience is *at least* as positive as it is negative if we can only set aside the negative conclusions of our ego.

FITNESS

I jog or race walk with Dana almost every day. Also, I lift weights and play basketball several times a week. I am very thankful that I live near an outdoor court. Regular exercise and eating lots of raw vegetables and fruits is another good way to stay away from the therapist's office.

COMMITMENT

I was in a powerful 6-day seminar (Fall of 87) and experienced a beautiful and frightening breakthrough in my work and personal life.

The seminar involved a strenuous hilly mile run each morning, a ropes course on one day, tasty healthy meals, and many confrontive hours in the seminar room. It was a fantastic experience.

On the 3rd day I was overwhelmed with feelings of love and commitment for my clients, friends and "loved ones." I realized that everyone was my loved one, to a depth I had not felt before. I experienced a significant jump in the power of my work and in my commitment to my clients. I realized I had to call Joe in Toronto and tell him that (and also tell him that when my Toronto seminar was over, he would be really sorry if people he loved had not gone through it).

I realized I had not been telling the truth about the power of the work I do. I have a gift for connecting people with this power in a simple fashion that they can see and apply in their everyday life. The thought of telling all this to Joe frightened me (even though he has been telling me this for years).

I finally called Joe with the above agenda and as soon as I heard his voice I had to tell him that I loved him. (Then I told him about my work.) I could hardly talk.

I cried and acknowledged my love for people quite a bit that week.

What shocked me was the day after my breakthrough I was emotionally dead—my old schizoid frightened depressed self of years past.

I asked myself, "What the hell is going on, you felt so great yesterday?" Suddenly, I could see it. My feelings of love and commitment were so strong, they terrorized me. I was afraid if I really showed the power of my work and my love, that I would be too far out on the limb —my heart would be too much on my sleeve —that people would laugh at me and ridicule me. (It is very hard to write this.)

So, ever since that sudden discovery, I have been going through cycles of intense positive feelings, then fear and deadness, and then re-creating my love and commitment for people. The love gets easier and easier and the fear gets weaker and weaker. My seminars and work and personal life will never be the same.

♥ 3-DAY LOVE AND FORGIVENESS SEMINARS AT MONROE PRISON

My Monroe work has a particular healing quality to it. It helps people connect with everyone on the planet as their brothers and sisters. This is very nitty-gritty-practical for people who have murdered and raped and/or been physically or sexually abused. (Most of my clients at Monroe have both committed violent crimes and been abused.)

In order to commit a violent crime, a person has to totally lose touch with (or deny) their connection to the person they are assaulting. Also, in order to maintain a judgment and/or rage or resentment towards the person(s) who abused or neglected them as children, a person (or inmate) must deny their deep connection to the abuser.

My work helps the inmates forgive everyone involved in these violent acts, including themselves and it helps them surrender to their deep connection with everyone involved. They end up experiencing, mind, body and spirit, that everytime they injure someone, they injure themselves. And everytime they help or love someone, they are helping and loving themselves.

To accomplish this, the inmate must go through a very intense experience whereby they re-live the traumatic event. Re-live is not too accurate a word because they are usually fully experiencing the event for the first time. (They denied or avoided the experience when they were in it the first time.) Not only do they fully experience the event as themselves, but they fully EXPERIENCE THE EVENT AS THE PERSON THEY KILLED OR RAPED. (Or if they were abused, they fully experience the event as the person who abused them, which is also necessary for the inmates' healing.) This is very vulnerable, difficult work.

Several inmates who have done this work say there is a peace and a completion to their lives that they have never felt before. They report sleeping the whole night through for the first time in as long as they can remember. One inmate said, "I would never admit this to anyone before, but for the first time since the murder, I don't see John's face when I go to sleep at night."

There are some other key aspects to this work that involve owning and integrating parts of themselves that they have denied, and projected onto the other person involved in the violent act. This is a powerful healing experience.

I do this work free for inmates, their families and volunteers. (It is additionally powerful because the administration allows relatives of inmates to attend these seminars.) We provide fruit, vegies, rolls, juice and self-help books for these seminars. My expenses run from $100 to $300 per 3-day seminar. If you would like to contribute juice, money or used self-help books, please give me a call or drop me a note 702- 11th East, Seattle, Washington 98102. 206/ 322-5785).

❤ LET'S EMPTY OUR PRISONS

A short story

You decided you want to "make a difference." It's your first day of volunteering at a pre-school containing children many of whom we suspect are physically and/or sexually abused outside of school. You are nervous and feel like you stick out. You wish your jeans and tennis shoes looked just a bit more worn or soiled. You approach a boy barely 3 who is trying to peel the new shelf liner off an old table top while he is kicking a playmate's leg under the table. As you get closer, the kicking gets meaner and he gives you a look that confronts you to your core. You sit beside him on a very small chair, pat his hand, smile and say, "what are you doing?" He pinches the back of your hand quite hard. You recoil and try to hide it, regroup, smile again and say, "let's be nice to each other" (but you notice that you wanted to slap him). He grabs his crotch and finally speaks to you: "Suck my pee pee."

You can hardly believe your ears. It's like a time warp where things are all turned around. You feel helpless, hopeless and speechless. You look at the teacher and it is as if she does not even know you are in the room. Her day has just started and already she seems to barely drag herself around. You had heard that volunteers last 2 weeks and right now that seems an eternity. Where do we go from here?

Albert Einstein said we all suffer from a sort of optical delusion. We act as if we are not connected to everything and everybody. This is especially what we do with the people who are filling up tomorrow's prisons and today's prisons.

If we want to empty our prisons, there are three populations of people that need a lot of "loving backbone" from us (us as individuals and "us" as a community).

1. The people currently in our correctional system

2. Our children currently being physically and sexually traumatized

3. The parents of the above children.

These populations need a great deal of love and attention. The dilemma is how do we love them and attend to them without reinforcing their destructive and addictive behavior. If it only takes a 3-year-old 2-1/2 minutes to make us feel like hitting him, we really have our hands full.

❤ What Is Loving Backbone?

Loving backbone is when you treat people with love and respect, do not let them abuse you or take advantage of you and do not let them provoke you into treating them like they are bad-evil-sick-crazy-stupid, (or other destructive retaliatory behavior on your part). All criminal behavior can be looked at like the 3-year-old who pinched you. In his world we are all either the abuser or the abusee. If you want to get close to him, he knows it is only a matter of time before you will mistreat him or at the very least, reject him. Your being nice to him makes him feel anxious and/or challenged. He gets a feeling of control and predictability, therefore, if he can rapidly manipulate you into abuse or rejection. His frightened little ego would already rather be right than happy.

❤ Our Ultimate Healing

Our ultimate healing as individuals and as a society, must include all of our brothers and sisters in prisons. Violence, drugs and greed are a significant part of our culture. Unfortunately, from a behavior modification standpoint, we offer big rewards for enterprising excellence in these areas. Most of us do not want to face the violence and greed in the dark corners of our hearts. We see it in criminals, deny it in ourselves and want to lock up the bad guys and throw away the key. These brothers and sisters are a part of us and so is their behavior. Our connection to their behavior is beyond our understanding so I encourage you, the reader, to be open to the possibility of what I am saying. Your openness can speed your healing and personal power.

When we learn to love our violent brothers and sisters it is nice for them but, on a deeper level, we will finally be loving a part of ourselves that we have been refusing to love our entire life. This makes no sense to your logical mind but your intuitive mind has a "feel" for what I am saying.

Loving people who have behaved violently does not condone or support their violence. Locking them up so they cannot hurt anyone can actually be an act of love. And loving them with backbone (i.e., structure and treatment opportunities) can actually decrease the chances that they will harm someone in the future. They have no happiness and peace of mind when they are hurting people. It might "give them a thrill" but it also makes them sick at heart.

I wish I could tell you more about our connection to this violence, but I am still learning about it myself.

❤ Shambhala Warriors

There is an ancient Tibetan prophecy about a powerful healing army (no uniforms, no weapons) that will evolve and emerge all over the planet around the year 2000. They are called Shambhala Warriors. A significant part of their power comes from their knowledge that the line between good and evil passes through the landscape of every human heart. The other aspect of their power comes from their balance of compassion and backbone.

Compassion without backbone will wear you out. You will end up as an exhausted doormat. Backbone without compassion is a cold, heartless, empty existence. Balance the two and you have a powerful person who can really make a difference in people's lives. We need to become Shambhala Warriors to empty our prisons.

"A human being is a part of the whole called by us 'Universe,' a part limited in time and space. He experiences himself, his thoughts and feelings as something separated from the rest--a kind of optical delusion of his consciousness. This delusion is a kind of prison for us, restricting us to our personal desires and to affection for a few persons nearest to us. Our task must be to free ourselves from this prison by widening our circle of compassion to embrace all living creatures and the whole nature in its beauty."

– Albert Einstein

International Love and Well Being Training Program

with Leonard Shaw, A.C.S.W.

For becoming a more empowering therapist, supervisor, boss, parent or mate

■ 1-3 year terms available
$1000 - 1800 per year

■ 1-3 month options for training in Toronto, Frankfurt, Copenhagen.
■ Convenient program for out-of-town people.

Apply or inquire: 206/ 322-5785

702 - 11th Ave E • Seattle, WA 98102

The International Psychotherapy Institution of Love and Well Being

❤ ORDER FORM

FOR LEONARD SHAW VHS VIDEO AND AUDIO CASSETTES

VHS Video 1 • $25.00 • Leonard being interviewed by Linda Stahl (Ch. 11 Tacoma) on Relationships and Little Mind-Big Mind

VHS Video 2 • $ 30.00 • Leonard leading a group of people through body relaxation, forgiveness, commitment and creative visualization

Audio Tape 1 • $12.00 • Leonard interviewed by Jennifer James plus sound track from Video 2, body relaxation, forgiveness, commitment and creative visualization

Audio Tape 2 • $12.00 • (Identical to pp. 1-75 of this *Love and Forgiveness* book) The Friday night introductory session of Leonard's 3-day seminar, i.e.: Love and Forgiveness, Little Mind-Big Mind

Book • *Love and Forgiveness: A workbook for Self Healing and Healing Relationships* • $10.00

Book	$10 x	_____
VHS 1	$25 x	_____
VHS 2	$30 x	_____
Audio 1	$12 x	_____
Audio 2	$12 x	_____

Subtotal _____

Handling + $2.00 ___$2.00___

Total _____

❤ *Love and Forgiveness*

Leonard M. Shaw, *ACSW, received his masters degree in psychiatric social work in 1963 and entered private practice 1966. Originally trained as a non-directive Freudian, he was heavily influenced by Carl Rogers' work in 1964 and Fritz Perls in 1967. After 11 years of studying, practicing and teaching Gestalt therapy, he started practicing what he now calls "Love-and-Forgiveness-Ego-Death-and-Surrender" therapy. However he struggled for a year before he surrendered to it. Ever since then he has been surrendering at deeper and deeper levels, much to the enrichment of his life and happiness. (The ego or "little mind" hates surrender.) His practice is in Seattle, Washington and he teaches at training centers in Toronto, Frankfurt and Copenhagen.*